# how2become

# Scottish Police Tests
# Information Handling

www.How2Become.com

by How2Become

Orders: Please contact How2Become Ltd, Suite 3, 40 Churchill Square Business Centre, Kings Hill, Kent ME19 4YU. You can also order via the email address info@How2Become.co.uk.

ISBN: 9781912370498

First published in 2018 by How2Become Ltd

2nd Edition

Typeset for How2Become Ltd by Anton Pshinka.

Attend a 1 Day Police Officer Training
Course by visiting:

# www.PoliceCourse.co.uk

Get more products for passing Scottish
Police selection at:

# www.How2Become.com

# CONTENTS

**Introduction to Your New Guide** ...............................................................6

**BEGINNER QUESTIONS** ...........................................................................9

**INTERMEDIATE** (Section 1) ....................................................................25

**INTERMEDIATE** (Section 2) ....................................................................53

**ADVANCED** (Section 1) ...........................................................................69

**ADVANCED** (Section 2) ...........................................................................81

**A Few Final Words...**................................................................................ 112

As part of this product you have received access to FREE online tests that will help you to pass the Scottish Police Tests!

To gain access, simply go to:

www.PsychometricTestsOnline.co.uk

For more information, please check out the following website:

www.How2Become.com

## INTRODUCTION TO YOUR NEW GUIDE

Welcome to *Scottish Police Information Handling Tests*. This is the ULTIMATE guide for passing the standard entrance test for the Scottish Police service. This guide has been designed to help you prepare for, and pass, the tough police officer selection process.

The selection process to join the police is highly competitive. Approximately 65,000 people apply to join the police every year. But what is even more staggering is that only approximately 7,000 of those applicants will be successful. You could view this as a worrying statistic, or alternatively you could view it that you are determined to be one of the 7,000 who are successful. Armed with this insider's guide, you have certainly taken the first step to passing the police officer selection process.

### About the Scottish Police Standard Entrance Test

The test is made up of three papers. There are three different versions of the test, therefore all applicants are allowed to sit the Standard Entrance Test (SET) a maximum of three times. The test covers:

- Language;
- Numbers;
- Information handling.

To help you get ready for the test, we've created sample Information Handling test questions for you to practice. You are allowed to use a calculator for these questions, and in the assessment.

Work through each test carefully before checking your answers at the end of the test.

There are plenty of test questions for you to try out within this guide which are relevant to the Information Handling test element of the selection process. Once you have completed the testing booklet you may wish to access our online police testing facility which you can find at:

# www.How2Become.com

Don't ever give up on your dreams; if you really want to become a police officer, then you can do it. The way to approach the police officer selection process is to embark on a programme of 'in-depth' preparation and this guide will help you to do exactly that.

The police officer selection process is not easy to pass. Unless, that is, you put in plenty of preparation. Your preparation must be focused in the right areas, and also be comprehensive enough to give you every chance of success. This guide will teach you how to be a successful candidate.

The way to pass the police officer selection process is to develop your own skills and experiences around the core competencies that are required to become a police officer. Many candidates who apply to join the police will be unaware that the core competencies even exist. This guide has been specifically designed to help you prepare for the Police Initial Recruitment Test that forms part of the assessment centre.

If you need any further help with any element of the police officer selection process including role play, written test and interview, then we offer a wide range of products to assist you. These are all available through our online shop www.How2Become.com. We also run a 1-day intensive Police Officer Course. Details are available at the website:

# www.PoliceCourse.co.uk

Once again, thank you for your custom and we wish you every success in your pursuit f becoming a police officer.

Work hard, stay focused, and secure your dream career.


**Best wishes,**

**The How2Become Team**

# BEGINNER
## QUESTIONS

Take a look at the questions below. There are 6 in total. These questions are set at a beginner level, and therefore you should find them really simple. We have designed these questions to help warm up your brain, and get you thinking mathematically, before you tackle the really challenging parts of this book!

### INFORMATION HANDLING TEST EXERCISE 1

Study the graph carefully then answer questions 1 - 6

## Shoplifting by month and location

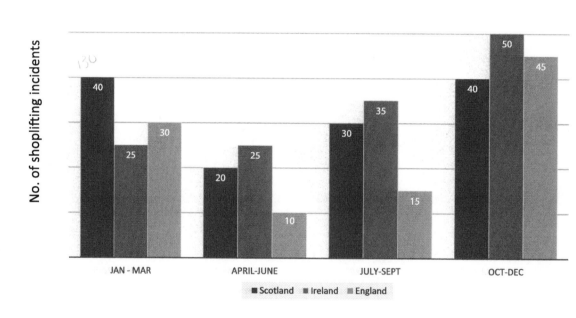

**Q1.** Between which months did the most shoplifting occur?

ANSWER: oct - dec

**Q2.** In which location did the most shoplifting occur?

ANSWER

**Q3.** In total, how many shoplifting incidents happened between Jan-Mar?

ANSWER

**Q4.** In total, how many shoplifting incidents happened in England?

ANSWER

**Q5.** From January to December, how many shoplifting incidents occurred in Scotland?

ANSWER

**Q6.** How many shoplifting incidents were there in total?

ANSWER

## INFORMATION HANDLING TEST EXERCISE 2

Study the graph carefully then answer questions 1 – 6

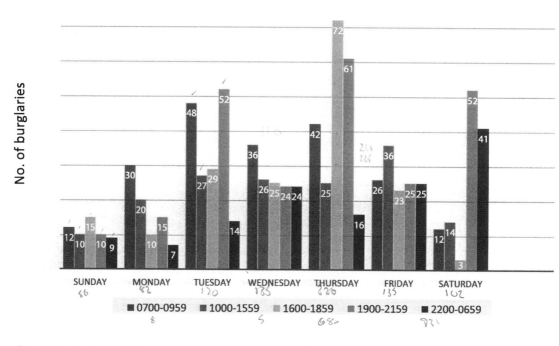

No. of burglaries by time and day

Q1. What day of the week are most burglaries committed?

ANSWER
> THURSDAY ✓

Q2. On what day are burglaries least likely to be committed?

ANSWER
> SUNDAY

**Q3.** How many burglaries are committed on Friday between 10:00 – 15:59?

ANSWER    36

**Q4.** On what day and between what times are burglaries mostly committed?

ANSWER    Thursday    1600-1859

**Q5.** How many burglaries are committed in total between the hours of 07:00 and 09:59?

ANSWER    206

**Q6.** How many burglaries were committed in total?

ANSWER    931

## INFORMATION HANDLING TEST EXERCISE 3

Study the graph carefully then answer questions 1 - 6

### Children's favourite animals

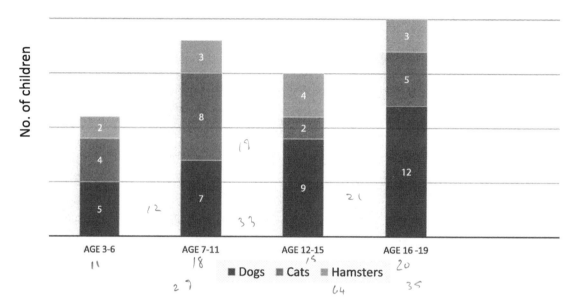

**Q1.** What is the most popular animal for children aged 7-11?

ANSWER    CATS

**Q2.** Amongst all ages, how many children chose cats as their favourite animal?

ANSWER    19

**Q3.** Which age group were hamsters least popular with?

ANSWER | 3 - 6

**Q4.** How many children took part in the survey?

ANSWER | 64

**Q5.** What is the least popular animal between the ages of 12 and 15?

ANSWER | CATS

**Q6.** What animal was most popular?

ANSWER | Dogs.

## INFORMATION HANDLING TEST EXERCISE 4

Study the graph carefully then answer questions 1 - 6

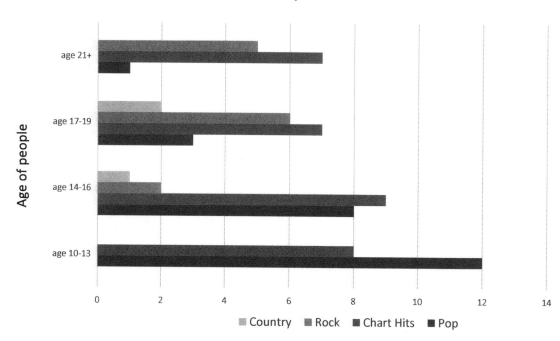

**Q1.** What was the most popular music choice between the ages of 14 and 16?

ANSWER CHoRiS

**Q2.** How many people liked country music?

ANSWER 3

**Q3.** In total, how many people liked pop music?

ANSWER | 24

**Q4.** What was the least popular music category?

ANSWER | Country

**Q5.** What was the most popular music category?

ANSWER | PoP CHRT.

**Q6.** Between the ages of 10 and 16, how many people liked chart hit music?

ANSWER | 17

## INFORMATION HANDLING TEST EXERCISE 5

Study the graph carefully then answer questions 1 - 6

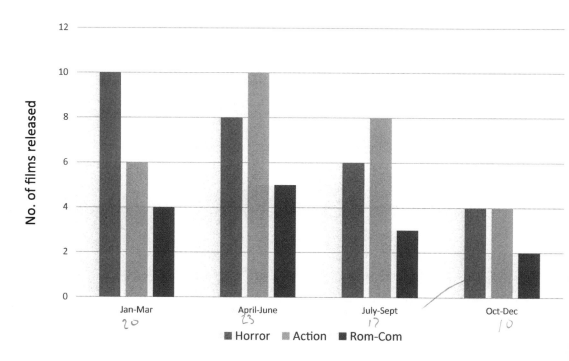

### No. of films released and the genre

No. of films released

Jan-Mar  2 0
April-June  2 3
July-Sept  1 7
Oct-Dec  1 0

■ Horror   ■ Action   ■ Rom-Com

**Q1.** What was the most commonly released film genre between the months of July and September?

ANSWER    ACTION

**Q2.** Over the 12 month period, what genre was released the least?

ANSWER    Rom com

**Q3.** How many action films were released between January and September?

ANSWER | 24

**Q4.** How many rom-com films were released in total?

ANSWER | 14

**Q5.** How many films were released between April and June?

ANSWER | 25

**Q6.** How many films were released in the 12 month period?

ANSWER | 70

## INFORMATION HANDLING TEST EXERCISE 6

Study the graph carefully then answer questions 1 - 6

## Types of crimes committed in a 12 month period

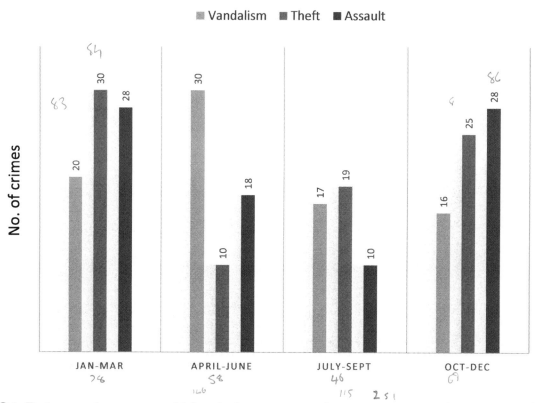

Q1. Between January and March, how many crimes were committed in total?

ANSWER | 78

Q2. How many crimes were committed between April and June?

ANSWER | 58

**Q3.** In total, how many crimes committed were vandalism?

ANSWER
83

**Q4.** How many assaults were there between January and September?

ANSWER
824   56.

**Q5.** How many crimes were committed in total?

ANSWER
251

**Q6.** What was the least committed crime?

ANSWER
Vandalism

**ANSWERS TO INFORMATION HANDLING** BEGINNER (SECTION 1)

## ANSWERS TO INFORMATION HANDLING TEST EXERCISE 1

Q1. Oct-Dec

Q2. Ireland

Q3. 95

Q4. 100

Q5. 130

Q6. 365

## ANSWERS TO INFORMATION HANDLING TEST EXERCISE 2

Q1. Thursday

Q2. Sunday

Q3. 36

Q4. Thursday between the hours of 1600 and 1859

Q5. 206

Q6. 916

## ANSWERS TO INFORMATION HANDLING TEST EXERCISE 3

Q1. Cats

Q2. 19

Q3. 3-6

Q4. 64

Q5. Cats

Q6. Dogs

## ANSWERS TO INFORMATION HANDLING TEST EXERCISE 4

Q1. Chart hits

Q2.  3

Q3. 24

Q4. Country

Q5. Chart hits

Q6. 17

## ANSWERS TO INFORMATION HANDLING TEST EXERCISE 5

Q1. Action

Q2. Rom-com

Q3.  24

Q4. 14

Q5. 23

Q6. 70

## ANSWERS TO INFORMATION HANDLING TEST EXERCISE 6

Q1. 78

Q2. 58

Q3. 83

Q4. 56

Q5. 251

Q6. Vandalism

# INTERMEDIATE
## SECTION 1

Now that you've warmed up, it's time to take on some trickier mathematics. In this section, you'll be given intermediate level questions. We've also included a few easy ones too, so you won't be jumping straight in the deep end! Have a go at both sections, and then check your answers against our ones.

## INFORMATION HANDLING TEST EXERCISE 1

Study the table carefully then answer questions 1 - 6

|  | After students leave school... | |
|---|---|---|
|  | Male | Female |
| College | 15000 | 10000 |
| University | 26000 | 45621 |
| Apprenticeship | 9000 | 1236 |
| Job | 8523 | 6354 |
| Total = | 58523 | 63211 |

152

**Q1.** How many people will be going to university?

26000 + 45621

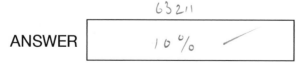

ANSWER   71621 /

**Q2.** What percentage of the total number of females will get a job after leaving school? Round your answer to the nearest whole percentage.

63211

ANSWER   10 %

**Q3.** Calculate how many more females than males will go to university, and then work out what percentage this is of the total number of people.

$$\begin{array}{r} ^3\cancel{4}^{1}5621 \\ -\ 26000 \end{array}$$   $19621$     ADD all PooPle up

ANSWER  $19621$ more.  $25$-$28\%$

**Q4.** In total, how many people will get an apprenticeship after leaving school?

ANSWER  $10236$

**Q5.** If you were female and leaving school, what are you most likely to do? Round your answer to the nearest whole percentage

ANSWER  UNIVERSITY  $25\%$.

**Q6.** What percentage of the total number of males did not attend college after leaving school? Round your answer to the nearest whole percentage.

ANSWER  $25\%$

## INFORMATION HANDLING TEST EXERCISE 2

Study the table carefully then answer questions 1 - 6

| Type of establishment | Secondary School | | University | |
|---|---|---|---|---|
| | Male | Female | Male | Female |
| Football | 256 | 62 | 398 | 162 |
| Dance | 165 | 268 | 169 | 368 |
| Boxing | 13    16 | 3 | 358    481 | 123 |
| Tennis | 98 | 68 | 160 | 76 |
| Rounders | 16 | 68 | 26 | 43 |
| Total = | 548 | 469 | 1111 | 772 |

548
1659

469
1241

1659

Football = 878
Dance = 970
Boxing = 497
Tennis = 402
Rounders = 153

2706
32

**Q1.** Which sport contained the biggest differential in male and female participants?

ANSWER | Football

**Q2.** How many more people played boxing in university compared to secondary school?

ANSWER | 465.

**Q3.** Work out the total number of people, and then calculate the percentage of these people that were male, and did not take dance at secondary school. Give your answer as a fraction.

ANSWER
| 2700 TOTAL |
| 1659 MALE |

✗

**Q4.** In total, how many people played the game of rounders?

ANSWER | 153 | ✓

**Q5.** What was the percentage increase in girls participating in sport, from secondary school to university? Round your answer to the nearest whole number/percentage.

ANSWER

**Q6.** In total, how many university students participated in any type of sport?

ANSWER

## INFORMATION HANDLING TEST EXERCISE 3

Study the table carefully then answer questions 1 - 6

| Holiday Preferences | Abroad | | | | In the UK | | | |
|---|---|---|---|---|---|---|---|---|
| | Spain | | America | | Butlins | | Lake District | |
| | Couples | Family | Couples | Family | Couples | Family | Couples | Family |
| All inclusive | 103 | 208 | 287 | 316 | 12 | 176 | 68 | 109 |
| Half board | 216 | 233 | 187 | 84 | 6 | 164 | 52 | 68 |
| Self Service | 36 | 95 | 79 | 65 | 1 | 76 | 36 | 49 |
| Total = | 355 | 536 | 553 | 465 | 19 | 416 | 156 | 226 |

*(Handwritten annotations: Spain Couples column — 311, 449; America Couples column — 603, 271; Butlins Couples column — 185, 170; Lake District Couples column — 177, 184)*

Total no. holidays = 2726

All inclusive = 1279
Half Board = 1010
Self Service = 437

**Q1.** In total, how many all-inclusive holidays were there?

ANSWER **1279**

**Q2.** If you were to go away abroad as a family, where are you most likely to go?

ANSWER **Spain**

**Q3.** How many half board holidays were there in the year?

ANSWER **920** ✗

**Q4.** If you were in a couple, are you more likely to go abroad or somewhere in the UK?

ANSWER  ABROAD

**Q5.** If you booked an all-inclusive holiday for your family in the UK, where are you most likely to go?

ANSWER 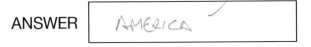 BUTLINS

**Q6.** Which holiday destination proved to be most popular?

ANSWER AMERICA

## INFORMATION HANDLING TEST EXERCISE 4

Study the table carefully then answer questions 1 - 6

| Type of establishment | Non-Indictable Offences | | | | | | | | Indictable Offences | | | | | | | |
| --- | --- | --- | --- | --- | --- | --- | --- | --- | --- | --- | --- | --- | --- | --- | --- | --- |
| | Male | | | | Female | | | | Male | | | | Female | | | |
| | Convicted | | Awaiting trial | | Convicted | | Awaiting trial | | Convicted | | Awaiting trial | | Convicted | | Awaiting trial | |
| | A | U21 | A | U21 | A | U21 | A | U21 | A | U21 | A | U21 | A | U21 | A | U21 |
| Prison | 485 | 180 | 68 | 52 | 153 | 35 | 12 | 19 | 208 | 189 | 12 | 16 | 96 | 103 | 7 | 19 |
| Youth institutions | | 86 | | 16 | | 73 | | 69 | | 64 | | 15 | | 52 | | 36 |
| Total: | 485 | 266 | 68 | 68 | 153 | 108 | 12 | 88 | 208 | 253 | 12 | 31 | 96 | 155 | 7 | 55 |

*(Handwritten annotations on table: 645, 579 near the first Male Convicted column; 18, 115 near Female Convicted; 397 near Indictable Male; 199 near Indictable Female)*

A = Adults
U21 – Under 21

Grand total = 2065

Prison = 1654
Youth Institutions = 411

Male = 1391
Female = 674

**Q1.** How many convicted young men aged under 21 are in prison for any type of offence?

ANSWER  *[handwritten: 275]*

**Q2.** In total, how many aged under 21 are in youth institutions?

ANSWER  *[handwritten: 150 a]*

**Q3.** How many adults are awaiting trial for non-indictable offences?

ANSWER | 80

**Q4.** How many females are awaiting trial?

ANSWER | 162

**Q5.** How many male adults, who are convicted prisoners, are there in total?

ANSWER | 683

**Q6.** How many more people are in prison as opposed to youth institutions?

ANSWER | 1069

665
188
397
198
─────
1842
3

86
77
64
52
─────
279
7

1842
279
1063

## INFORMATION HANDLING TEST EXERCISE 5

Study the table carefully then answer questions 1 - 6

| | Convicted | | | | Non - Convicted | | | |
|---|---|---|---|---|---|---|---|---|
| | Male | | Female | | Male | | Female | |
| | A | U21 | A | U21 | A | U21 | A | U21 |
| Theft | 166 | 265 | 68 | 96 | 46 | 26 | 24 | 15 |
| Drug Offences | 356 | 254 | 126 | 85 | 12 | 4 | 4 | 3 |
| Motoring | 369 | 369 | 49 | 109 | 56 | 65 | 31 | 45 |
| Criminal Damage | 256 | 251 | 169 | 56 | 43 | 15 | 2 | 13 |
| Sexual Offences | 235 | 96 | 19 | 10 | 5 | 3 | 2 | 1 |
| Fraud | 357 | 23 | 120 | 8 | 13 | 11 | 16 | 10 |
| Total = | 1739 | 1258 | 551 | 364 | 175 | 124 | 79 | 87 |

*(handwritten annotations overlaid on table: 610, 73%, 211, 158 in Male columns; 72, 16, 121, 197, 58, 6, 24, 101 in Non-Convicted Male columns; 29, 7, 76, 15, 5, 26 in Female A column)*

*(handwritten below totals: 2, 1239 / 2992, 915 / 2992, 299, 168, 3911, 367, 3650, 3911, 3650)*

Grand Total = 4377

Convictions = 3912
Non Convictions = 465

**Q1.** In total, how many convictions were there for drug offences?

ANSWER  *821*

**Q2.** Work out which crime received the highest total non-conviction rate, and then work out the percentage increase in this number to the total conviction rate in the same category. Round your answer to the nearest whole number/percent.

ANSWER  *Motoring / 197 Non Conviction / 896 Conviction*

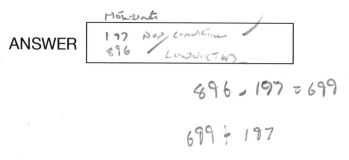

*896 - 197 = 699*

*699 ÷ 197*

**Q3.** How many convictions were there in total for male adults?

ANSWER | 1739

**Q4.** If you are aged under 21 and female, what is the most likely offence that you will be convicted for?

ANSWER | MOTORING

**Q5.** In total, how many adults were linked with fraud based offences?

ANSWER | 29

**Q6.** How many more convictions were there as opposed to non-convicted offences?

ANSWER | 3650

## INFORMATION HANDLING TEST EXERCISE 6

Study the table carefully then answer questions 1 - 6

| Job Occupation | England | | Scotland | | Ireland | | Wales | |
|---|---|---|---|---|---|---|---|---|
| | Male | Female | Male | Female | Male | Female | Male | Female |
| Police officer | 165 | 251 | 150 | 76 | 30 | 26 | 45 | 13 |
| Teacher | 98 | 208 | 96 | 120 | 23 | 64 | 36 | 65 |
| Musician | 206 | 121 | 126 | 35 | 169 | 13 | 76 | 9 |
| Doctor | 365 | 68 | 43 | 35 | 46 | 26 | 16 | 15 |
| Sales | 156 | 65 | 56 | 32 | 54 | 18 | 62 | 36 |
| Total = | 990 | 713 | 471 | 298 | 322 | 147 | 235 | 138 |

Grand Total = 3314

No. of Police officers = 756
No. of Teachers = 710
No. of Musicians = 755
No. of Doctors = 614
No. of Sales = 479

**Q1.** Which occupation saw the biggest differential between male and female employment figures?

ANSWER  Doctor.

**Q2.** How many police officers are there across England and Scotland?

ANSWER  642

**Q3.** What is the total number of English males, who do not work in the medical or sales industries. Give your answer as a fraction (in its simplest form) of the total number of people surveyed.         3314        46)

ANSWER

**Q4.** In total, how many people work in sales?

ANSWER    476

**Q5.** Which country saw the lowest difference in employment figures between the two genders?

ANSWER    IRDLAND ✗

**Q6.** In which country, and for which occupation and gender, can you find the largest differential between that and the grand total for the country's gender pool?

**For example:**

In Ireland there are 30 males working as a police officer, and 322 males surveyed in total. Therefore the differential is 292.

ANSWER

## INFORMATION HANDLING TEST EXERCISE 7

Study the table carefully then answer questions 1 - 6

| Drug Use | England | | | | Scotland | | | |
|---|---|---|---|---|---|---|---|---|
| | Male | | Female | | Male | | Female | |
| | A | U21 | A | U21 | A | U21 | A | U21 |
| Cannabis | 358 | 165 | 163 | 113 | 132 | 76 | 45 | 33 |
| Heroin | 153 | 75 | 76 | 65 | 103 | 56 | 16 | 12 |
| Cocaine | 136 | 16 | 131 | 35 | 86 | 35 | 11 | 9 |
| Other | 56 | 35 | 32 | 12 | 32 | 12 | 9 | 6 |
| | 703 | 291 | 402 | 225 | 353 | 179 | 81 | 60 |

Total Drug Use: 2294

Cannabis = 1085
Heroin = 556
Cocaine = 459
Other = 194

**Q1.** How many people used drugs in total?

ANSWER    2294

**Q2.** What location saw the least use of drugs?

ANSWER    SCOTLAND

**Q3.** How many people used heroin in England?

ANSWER

228

**Q4.** In England and Scotland, how many people used cocaine?

ANSWER
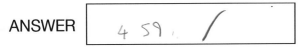
4 59

**Q5.** What drug was most popular to use in England, if you were under 21 and female?

ANSWER
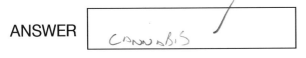
CANNABIS

**Q6.** What drug was most popular to use in Scotland if you were an adult and male?

ANSWER
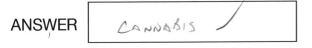
CANNABIS

## INFORMATION HANDLING TEST EXERCISE 8

Study the table carefully then answer questions 1 - 6

| Intoxication | Alcohol | | Cigarettes | |
|---|---|---|---|---|
| | Male | Female | Male | Female |
| Recommended | 12 | 63 | - | - |
| 2-3 (units/per) | 36 | 23 | 26 | 36 |
| 4-5 (units/per) | 49 | 36 | 64 | 45 |
| 5+ | 56 | 26 | 59 | 32 |
| Total = | 153 | 148 | 149 | 113 |

201

262

**Q1.** In total, how many people drink alcohol?

ANSWER      301

**Q2.** How many females have cigarettes?

ANSWER      113

**Q3.** In total, how many men drink 4-5 units of alcohol?

ANSWER      49

**Q4.** In total, how many women smoke 4-5 cigarettes?

ANSWER      32

**Q5.** How many people in total use cigarettes and/or alcohol?

ANSWER

463

**Q6.** For females, what is the most likely amount they would drink in regards to alcohol?

ANSWER

4-5 units

## INFORMATION HANDLING TEST EXERCISE 9

Study the table carefully then answer questions 1 - 6

| Location | Teenage pregnancy regarding location | | | | | | | |
|---|---|---|---|---|---|---|---|---|
| | England | | Italy | | Spain | | Wales | |
| | 13-16 | 17-20 | 13-16 | 17-20 | 13-16 | 17-20 | 13-16 | 17-20 |
| Keeping the baby | 36 | 63 | 11 | 23 | 19 | 23 | 2 | 3 |
| Abortion | 12 | 13 | 6 | 13 | 16 | 3 | 0 | 1 |
| Adoption | 16 | 16 | 8 | 9 | 4 | 5 | 1 | 1 |
| Undecided | 43 | 23 | 16 | 11 | 18 | 19 | 1 | 2 |
| Total = | 107 | 115 | 41 | 56 | 57 | 50 | 4 | 7 |

Total no. of pregnancies = 437

England = 222

Italy = 97

Spain = 107

Wales = 11

**Q1.** Where would you need to be living in order to have the least chance of teenage pregnancy?

ANSWER   WALES

**Q2.** What location has the highest level of teenage pregnancy?

ANSWER   ENGLAND

**Q3.** How many people in the survey wanted to keep their baby from England and Spain?

ANSWER | 141 ✓

**Q4.** In total, how many people wanted to give their baby up for adoption?

ANSWER | 60

**Q5.** If you were living in Spain, at what age group are you most likely to get pregnant?

ANSWER | 13-16

**Q6.** How many people living in England wanted to keep their baby?

ANSWER | 99

## INFORMATION HANDLING TEST EXERCISE 10

Study the table carefully then answer questions 1 - 6

| | Male | | | | Female | | | |
|---|---|---|---|---|---|---|---|---|
| | 18-25 | 26-35 | 36-49 | 50+ | 18-25 | 26-35 | 36-49 | 50+ |
| Toyota | 103 | 196 | 186 | 276 | 265 | 268 | 168 | 150 |
| Ford | 206 | 186 | 275 | 46 | 356 | 268 | 163 | 96 |
| Mercedes | 23 | 96 | 68 | 196 | 2 | 23 | 68 | 42 |
| Renault | 352 | 172 | 165 | 23 | 67 | 154 | 86 | 41 |
| BMW | 12 | 32 | 68 | 146 | 3 | 35 | 76 | 32 |
| Vauxhall | 269 | 126 | 112 | 136 | 109 | 120 | 162 | 106 |
| Other | 5 | 8 | 13 | 21 | 3 | 23 | 32 | 36 |
| Total = | 970 | 816 | 887 | 844 | 805 | 891 | 755 | 503 |

Grand total = 6471

**Q1.** If you are a 23 year old female, what car are you most likely to get?

ANSWER    ford

**Q2.** What car is the most popular with men?

ANSWER    Toyota

**Q3.** In which brand of car can you find the biggest numerical differential, between male and female owners?

ANSWER    a

**Q4.** In which age and gender does the modal number for this set of data appear the most frequently?

ANSWER

**Q5.** In which age range and gender would you find the lowest scoring type of car?

ANSWER | Femnub 18-25

**Q6.** If you were a 50 year old man, what car are you most likely to have?

ANSWER | Toyota.

## ANSWERS TO INFORMATION HANDLING INTERMEDIATE (SECTION 1)

### EXERCISE 1

**Q1.** 71261

EXPLANATION = 26000 + 45261 = 71261

**Q2.** 10%

EXPLANATION = There are 63211 females. To calculate the percentage that got a job, divide 6354 by 63211 to give you 0.10052, then x this by 100 = 10.05%. Rounded to the nearest whole percentage this gives you 10%

**Q3.** 16%

EXPLANATION = There are 121,734 people in total. There were 19621 more females than males who went to university. 19621/121,734 = 0.1611 x 100 = 16.11. Rounded to the nearest percentage gives you 16%

**Q4.** 10236

EXPLANATION = 9000 + 1236 = 10236

**Q5.** University

EXPLANATION = 45621 females left school and went to university, which was by far the largest figure in the whole table.

**Q6.** 74%

EXPLANATION = 43523 males did not attend college after leaving school. Divided by the total number of males, this = 74.36%. Rounded to the nearest whole percentage gives you 74%.

### EXERCISE 2

**Q1.** Football

EXPLANATION = In football the differential between male and female participants was 430.

In dance the differential between male and female participants was 302.

In boxing the differential between male and female participants was 245.

In tennis the differential between male and female participants was 114.

In rounders the differential between male and female participants was 69.

**Q2.** 465

EXPLANATION = There were 481 people who participated in boxing at university. There were just 16 people who participated in boxing at secondary school. 481 – 16 = 465

**Q3.** 747/1450

EXPLANATION = There were 2900 people in total. 1494 of these were male, and did not take dance at secondary school. Therefore, the fraction is 1494/2900. Simplify this by dividing each number by 2, to give you 747/1450.

**Q4.** 153

EXPLANATION = 16 + 68 + 26 + 43 = 153

**Q5.** 65%

EXPLANATION = First, work out the increase between girls participating in sport at secondary school, and at university. 772 – 469 = 303. Then divide 303 by 469, to get 0.646. x 100 = 64.6. Rounded to the nearest whole percentage this = 65%

**Q6.** 1883

EXPLANATION = 1111 + 772 = 1883.

## EXERCISE 3

**Q1.** 1279

EXPLANATION = 103 + 208 + 287 + 316 + 12 + 176 + 68 + 109 = 1279

**Q2.** Spain

EXPLANATION = There were 536 family holidays abroad to Spain, compared to 465 family holidays to America.

**Q3.** 1010

EXPLANATION = 216 + 233 + 187 + 84 + 6 + 164 + 52 + 68 = 1010

**Q4.** Abroad

EXPLANATION = There were 908 couple holidays abroad, compared to 175 couple holidays in the UK.

**Q5.** Butlins

EXPLANATION = There were 176 all-inclusive holidays to Butlins, in the UK, compared to 109 all-inclusive holidays to the Lake District, also in the UK.

**Q6.** USA

EXPLANATION = USA was the most popular holiday destination, with 1018 holidays, compared to second place Spain, which had 891 holidays.

## EXERCISE 4

**Q1.** 369

EXPLANATION = 180 + 189 = 369

**Q2.** 411

EXPLANATION = 86 + 16 + 73 + 69 + 64 + 15 + 52 + 36 = 411

**Q3.** 80

EXPLANATION = 68 + 12 = 80 (don't forget to include both men and women)

**Q4.** 162

EXPLANATION = 69 + 19 + 19 + 36 + 12 + 7 = 162

**Q5.** 693

EXPLANATION = 485 + 208

**Q6.** 1243

EXPLANATION = 1654 − 411 = 1243

## EXERCISE 5

**Q1.** 821

EXPLANATION = 356 + 254 + 126 + 85 = 821

**Q2.** 355%

EXPLANATION = The category with the highest total non-convictions was Motoring, with 197 non-convictions. There were 896 convictions in the same category. To work out the percentage increase, calculate 896 − 197 = 699, then divide 699 by 197 to get 3.54822. Multiply this by 100 to reach

354.8, rounded up to the nearest whole number = 355%

**Q3.** 1739

EXPLANATION = 166 + 356 + 369 + 256 + 235 + 357 = 1739

**Q4.** Motoring

EXPLANATION = In the category of females under the age of 21, the highest scoring section is motoring, with 109 offences.

**Q5.** 506

EXPLANATION = 357 + 120 + 13 + 16 = 506

**Q6.** 3447

EXPLANATION = 1739 + 1258 + 551 + 364 = 3912

175 + 124 + 79 + 87 = 465

3912 − 465 = 3447


## EXERCISE 6

**Q1.** Musician

EXPLANATION = There were 577 male musicians, compared to just 178 female musicians, with a differential of 399 – the largest in the table.

**Q2.** 642

EXPLANATION = 165 + 251 + 150 + 76 = 642

**Q3.** 469/3314

EXPLANATION = 165 + 98 + 206 = 469.

There were 3314 people surveyed in total, so 469/3314. This fraction cannot be simplified, so the answer is 469/3314.

**Q4.** 479

EXPLANATION = 156 + 65 + 56 + 32 + 54 + 18 + 62 + 36 = 479

**Q5.** Wales

EXPLANATION =

The difference in gender employment figures for England was 277.

The difference in gender employment figures for Scotland was 193.

The difference in gender employment figures for Ireland was 175.

The difference in gender employment figures for Wales was 97.

Therefore, the answer is Wales.

**Q6.** England, Male, Teacher

EXPLANATION = There are 98 male teachers in England. When compared to the total figure of males surveyed in England – 990, this makes a differential of 892, which is the largest in the table.

## EXERCISE 7

**Q1.** 2294

EXPLANATION = As shown by the key at the bottom, there were 2,294 drug users in total.

**Q2.** Scotland

EXPLANATION = There were 673 people in Scotland who used drugs, compared to England's 1621.

**Q3.** 369

EXPLANATION = 153 + 75 + 76 + 65 = 369

**Q4.** 459

EXPLANATION = 136 + 16 + 131 + 35 + 86 + 35 + 11 + 9 = 459

**Q5.** Cannabis

EXPLANATION = Cannabis was the most popular drug for females aged under 21, in England, with 113 people in this category using it.

**Q6.** Cannabis.

EXPLANATION = Cannabis was the most popular drug for adult males in Scotland, with 132 people in this category using it.

## EXERCISE 8

**Q1.** 301

EXPLANATION = 153 + 148 = 301

**Q2.** 113

EXPLANATION = 36 + 45 + 32 = 113

**Q3.** 49

EXPLANATION = As indicated by the table, 49 men drink 4-5 units of alcohol.

**Q4.** 45

EXPLANATION = As indicated by the table, 45 women smoke 4-5 cigarettes.

**Q5.** 563

EXPLANATION = 153 + 148 + 149 + 113 = 563

**Q6.** Recommended

EXPLANATION = There are 63 women who drink the recommend amount of alcohol, which is the highest figure in this section of the table.

**EXERCISE 9**

**Q1.** Wales

EXPLANATION = Wales has by far the lowest rate of teenage pregnancy, with just 11 pregnancies.

**Q2.** England

EXPLANATION = England has a substantially higher rate of teenage pregnancy than any other country in the table, with 222 pregnancies.

**Q3.** 141

EXPLANATION = 36 + 63 + 19 + 23 = 141

**Q4.** 60

EXPLANATION = 16 + 16 + 8 + 9 + 4 + 5 + 1 + 1 = 60

**Q5.** 13-16

EXPLANATION = There were 57 pregnancies in the age bracket 13-16 in Spain, compared to 50 in the age bracket 17-20.

**Q6.** 99

EXPLANATION = 36 + 63 = 99.

## EXERCISE 10

**Q1.** Ford

EXPLANATION = By far the most popular choice for females between the ages of 18-25 (which 23 falls into) was Ford – with 356 people.

**Q2.** Toyota

EXPLANATION = Toyota is the most popular choice with men overall, with 761 men using this as their choice of car.

**Q3.** Renault

EXPLANATION = 352 + 172 + 165 + 23 = 712.

67 + 154 + 86 + 41 = 348

712 – 348 = 364

**Q4.** Female, 26-35

EXPLANATION = The modal number is the number which appears the most frequently. In this case, the modal number is 23. 23 appears 4 times in this table, but occurs twice in females aged 26-35, making this the answer.

**Q5.** Female, 18-25, other

EXPLANATION = The lowest scoring car was 'other' with just 3 people, and can be found in females, 18-25.

**Q6.** Toyota

EXPLANATION = If you are a 50-year-old man then you are most likely to have a Toyota. Toyota was the highest scoring car in this category, with 276.

# INTERMEDIATE
## SECTION 2

## INFORMATION HANDLING TEST EXERCISE 1

Study the information in the list below. The following is an extract from the catalogue of books on sale at a book shop.

### Catalogue page for books

Code 123: *Youth Studies*; Blackman, R. Paperback. £24.99 ISBN 0-3658-4532

Code 124: *Introduction to Youth Culture*; Downey, T. [download] £18.99 ISBN 0-4698-6983

Code 125: *Youth Culture*; Walker, P. Paperback. £27.99 ISBN 0-1355-4384

Code 126: *Youth Culture and Deviance*; Downey, R. Hardback. £38.99 ISBN 0-9534-4381

Code 127: *Youth and Subcultures*; Lewis, T. Hardback. £26.99 ISBN 0-9647-2535

Code 128: *Youth – Stereotypes and Subcultures*; Franklin, J. Hardback. £37.99 ISBN 0-3258-7216

Code 129: *The Problematic Youth of Today*; Johnson, M. Paperback. £27.99 ISBN 0-6589-1234

Code 130: *Theories of Youth Culture*; Davidson, H. Hardback. £15.50 ISBN 0-7693-3586

Code 131: *Understanding Contemporary Youth*; Michaels, D. Hardback. £12.99 ISBN 0-3635-6521

Code 132: *Understanding Contemporary Youth in Modern Society*; Michaels, D. Hardback. £18.99 ISBN 0-3635-6522

### Complete the missing entries in this customer order list

| Entry Code | Price | Title | Author | Binding | ISBN |
|---|---|---|---|---|---|
| 127 | 26.99 | Youth and subcultures | Lewis T | Hardback | 0-9647 2535 |
| 130 | £15.50 | Theories of Youth culture | Davidson H | Hardback | 0-7693-3586 |
| 131 | £12.99 | Understanding Contemporary Youth | Michaels, D | Hardback back | 0-3635-6521 |
| 123 | £24.99 | Youth Studies | Blackman R | Paper back | 0-3658 4532 |
| 124 | 18.99 | Introduction to Youth culture | Downey, T | [download] | 0-4698 6983 |

## INFORMATION HANDLING TEST EXERCISE 2

Study the information in the list below. The following is an extract from the catalogue on a clothing website.

### Catalogue on a clothing website

Code 110:  Sophie May Backless Dress. White/Black. Size 10. £45.00 Ref no: 2569873

Code 111:  Lilly Rose Sequinned Dress. Pink/ Black. Size 8. £25.99 Ref no: 4567823

Code 112:  Summer Backless Prom Dress. Aqua. Size 12. £20.00 Ref no. 4258793

Code 113:  Hannah May Long Sleeved Dress. Red. Size 12. £20.00 Ref no. 4632895

Code 114:  Rosie Jane Bodycon Dress. Pink. Size 10. £10.00 Ref no. 7456325

Code 115:  Fitted Alter neck Dress. Flowery. Size 6. £15.00 Ref no. 4796258

Code 116:  Lucy May Maxi Dress. Blue/Silver. Size 8. £16.99 Ref no. 7432686

Code 117:  Tailor made strapless dress. Black. Size 10. £9.99 Ref no. 1236852

Code 118:  Juliette swirl Bodycon dress. Green. Size 12. £12.99 Ref no, 9635423

### Complete the missing entries in this customer order list

| Code | Name | Colour | Size | Price | Ref No. |
|---|---|---|---|---|---|
| Code 110 |  | White/black |  |  |  |
|  | Summer backless prom dress |  |  | £20.00 |  |
| Code 114 |  |  | 10 |  | 7456325 |
|  | Tailor made strapless dress | Black |  |  |  |
|  |  |  |  | £12.99 | 9635423 |

## INFORMATION HANDLING TEST EXERCISE 3

Study the information in the list below. The following is an extract from an Avon Book catalogue.

### Avon Book Catalogue

Item 16:  Black Mascara. Black. £5.99. Ref no. 14563259. pg. 5

Item 19:  Shimmery Lip gloss. Peach. £3.99. Ref no. 45339521. pg. 7

Item 20:  Shimmery Lip gloss. Pink. £3.99. Ref no. 45339522. pg. 7

Item 21:  Shimmery Lip gloss. Clear. £3.99. Ref no. 45339523. pg. 7

Item 25:  Shine and Clear Powder. Translucent. £3.99. Ref no. 56985326. pg. 9

Item 32:  Bristled foundation brush. £11.99. Ref no. 45692369. pg. 12

Item 33:  Powder Brush. £15.99. Ref no. 46691238. pg. 12

Item 38:  NEW! Magic Eyeliner. Black. £8.99. Ref no. 49684532. pg. 14

Item 39:  NEW! Magic Eyeliner. Brown. £8.99. Ref no. 49684533. pg. 14

Item 40:  Shimmery Royal Blue eye palette. £10.99. Ref no. 78936234. pg.14

### Complete the missing entries in this customer order list

| Item no. | Product | Colour | Price | Ref no. | Page |
|---|---|---|---|---|---|
| 16 | Black mascara | | | 14563259 | |
| | Shine and Clear Powder | | £3.99 | | 9 |
| 20 | | Pink | £3.99 | | |
| | | | £3.99 | 45339523 | 7 |
| 40 | | Royal blue | | | 14 |

## INFORMATION HANDLING TEST EXERCISE 4

Study the information in the list below. The following is an extract from a Football boot embroideries sheet.

### Football boot embroideries Sheet (£2 per letter per boot)

Item 1:   James. Hyperspeed IX football boots. Size 11. 465892-06-130 Green. Both boots. £20.

Item 2:   e.r.d. Prowler Nimbus boots. Size 9. 659846-15-650. Black. Left boot. £6

Item 3:   White. Stallion Promptus football boots. Size 8. 698564-07-450. White. Both boots. £20.

Item 4:   D.P. Stallion Cutlass football boots. Size 9. 469256-15-650. Black. Both boots. £8.

Item 5:   Lewis. Stallion Azrael football boots. Size 10. 259873-07-456. White. Right boot. £10.

Item 6:   Marianne. Lightningbolt Jet-Heel football boots. Size 5. 469872-18-652. Pink. Both boots. £32.

Item 7:   T.J. Stallion Promptus football boots. Size 10. 698564-15-450. White. Both boots. £8.

Item 8:   JG8. Prowler Nimbus boots. Size 7. 659846-03-452. Blue. Both boots. £12

### Complete the missing entries for this boot embroidery sheet

| Item no: | Name on boots: | Boots: | Size: | Code: | Colour: | Right/Left/ Both boots: | Price: |
|---|---|---|---|---|---|---|---|
| | D.P | | 9 | 469256-15-650 | | both | |
| 3 | | Stallion Promptus | 8 | | White | | £20 |
| 5 | Lewis | | | | White | Right boot | |
| | | Stallion Promptus | 10 | | White | | |
| | JG8 | | | 659846-03-452 | | | £12 |

## INFORMATION HANDLING TEST EXERCISE 5

Study the information in the list below. The following is an extract from a 'printing on the back of football shirts' sheet.

### Printing on the back of football shirts sheet

Item 1: South Ficshire football shirt. Premiership. 23659779. White. Curved. David. 8.

Item 2: England football shirt. England, Away. 65987245. Navy. Straight. Jamie. 4.

Item 3: North Ficshire football shirt. Premiership. 45698523. Navy. Curved. Marianne. 10.

Item 4: England football shirt. England, Home. 65987426. White. Curved. Madison. 12

Item 5: South Ficshire football shirt. Premiership. 25697523. White. Straight. Big Daddy. 50.

Item 6: South Ficshire football shirt. Premiership. 46584563. White. Curved. Stephen. 16.

Item 7: England football shirt. England, Home. 46872587. White. Straight. Elizabeth. 21.

Item 8: North Ficshire football shirt. Premiership. 46987412. Navy. Curved. Oliver. 10

### Complete the missing entries from this football shirt printing sheet

| Item no. | Team: | Premiership/ England: | Home/ Away: | Code: | Colour: | Straight/ Curved | Name printed: | Age printed: |
|---|---|---|---|---|---|---|---|---|
| 2 | | | Away | | | | Jamie | 4 |
| | North Ficshire | Premiership | - | 45698523 | Navy | Curved | | |
| | | Premiership | - | | White | | Big Daddy | |
| 7 | | | Home | | | Straight | | 21 |
| 4 | | | Home | 65987426 | | | Madison | |

# INFORMATION HANDLING TEST EXERCISE 6

Study the information in the list below. The following is an extract from a catalogue of health and safety books.

## Catalogue of health and safety books:

Code 263: *Health and safety: an introduction.* Jackson, J. Hardcopy. JJPB Books: London. £29.99. ISBN 0-4569-7596

Code 264: *An introduction to safety in the workplace.* Harrison, A. Paperback. Graves: New York. £35.99. ISBN 0-7896-4236

Code 265: *Safety in action.* Friend, J. Hardcopy. JJPB Books: London. £30.00. ISBN 0-4526-8523

Code 266: *Making sure your workplace is a safe place to work.* Reynolds, L. Paperback. JJPB Books: London. £22.99. ISBN 0-3698-7412

Code 267: *An introduction to rules and regulations of work environments.* Anderson, A. Paperback. Graves: New York. ISBN £45.99. 0-5698-5478

Code 268: *Health procedures and safety guidelines.* Richards, E. Hardcopy. JJPB Books: London. £15.99. ISBN 0-1298-7836

Code 269: *All you need to know about your workplace.* Brown. E. Paper back. JJPB Books: London. £16.99. ISBN 0-1285-6539

Code 270: *Guidelines for your workplace.* Powley, D. Hardcopy. New Paper Books: London. £24.99. ISBN 0-3596-0056

Code 271: *The Workplace: Rules and Regulations.* Ericson, P. Paper back. Graves: New York. £16.99. ISBN 0-0069-5690

## Complete the missing entries for this customer order sheet

| Code: | Title: | Author: | Copy: | Publisher: | Location: | Price: | ISBN: |
|---|---|---|---|---|---|---|---|
| | | Harrison, A | | Palgrave | | £35.99 | 0-7896-4236 |
| 265 | | Friend, J | Hardcopy | | London | £30.00 | |
| | Health procedures and safety guidelines | | Hardcopy | | London | | |
| | | Powley, D | | Pearson Education | | | 0-3596-0056 |
| 271 | The Workplace: Rules and Regulations | | Paperback | | New York | £16.99 | |

## INFORMATION HANDLING TEST EXERCISE 7

Study the information in the list below. The following is an extract from an online Dress Shopping Catalogue.

### Online Dress Shopping Catalogue

Item 11:  Silver Sequin Dress. Black/Silver. Size 10. Was £65.00. Now £30.00. Order no. 4652365

Item 12:  Camilla Red sequinned skirt. Red/Black. Size 12. Was £30.00. Now £15.00. Order no. 4985232

Item 13:  Cassandra Black fitted dress. Black. Size 8. Was £65.00. Now £45.00. Order no. 9635875

Item 14:  Lilly flowered white halter neck top. White/flowery. Size 10. Was £30.00. Now £12.00. Order no. 4569852

Item 15:  Roxy May Gold flare skirt. Gold/Black. Size 12. Was £50.00. Now £20.00. Order no. 9635891

Item 16:  Lilly May Detailed Long sleeved black dress. Black. Size 10. Was £70.00. Now £35.00. Order no. 3596547

Item 17:  Phoebe Rose Prom dress. Blue. Size 8. Was £90.00. Now £45.00 Order no. 6596325

Item 18:  Sandra Sequined Silver Dress. Silver. Size 8. Was £70.00. Now £30.00. Order no. 9633687

### Complete the missing entries for this customers order form

| Item no: | Product: | Colour: | Size: | Was: | Now: | Order no. |
|---|---|---|---|---|---|---|
| 12 | | Red/Black | 12 | | £15.00 | |
| | Lilly flowered white halter neck top | | 10 | | | 4569852 |
| | | Gold/Black | | £50.00 | £20.00 | 9635891 |
| 17 | Phoebe Rose Prom Dress | | 8 | | £45.00 | |
| | | Black | | £65.00 | £45.00 | |

## INFORMATION HANDLING TEST EXERCISE 8

Study the information in the list below. The following is an extract from a catalogue from a DVD and Blu-Ray shop.

**Catalogue from a DVD and Blu-Ray shop**

Item 159: DVD. Bald Eagle Blues. Director: Melissa May Mora. £9.99.
Ref no. 3633256

Item 160: Blu-ray. The Gremlin in the Grotto. Director:
Mickey Cohen. £12.99. Ref no. 5968759

Item 161: DVD. The Gremlin in the Grotto. Director: Chris
Columbus John Taylor. £9.99. Ref no. 2366984

Item 162: DVD. Ashen Nightmare. Director: Kelly Dickinson. £5.99.
Ref no. 4568798

Item 163: DVD. The Last Titan. Director: Jennifer Grant. £8.99. Ref no.
4698677

Item 164: Blu-ray. The Last Titan. Director: Jennifer Grant. £12.99. Ref no.
4566598

Item 165: DVD. War Without End. Director: John Taylor. £10.99. Ref
no. 3652206

Item 166: Blu-ray. War Without End. Director: John Taylor. £15.99.
Ref no. 6986326

**Complete the missing entries for this customers order list**

| Item no: | DVD/ Blu-ray | Film title: | Director: | Price: | Ref no: |
|---|---|---|---|---|---|
| 160 | | | Mickey Cohen | £12.99 | 5968759 |
| | DVD | | Mickey Cohen | | 2366984 |
| | DVD | The Last Titan | | £8.99 | |
| 166 | | | John Taylor | | |

## INFORMATION HANDLING TEST EXERCISE 9

Study the information in the list below. The following is an extract from a men's fashion clothing website.

### Men's fashion clothing website

Code 125:  Men's tailor made fitted jacket. Black. Size small. £25.99. Ref no. 46356978

Code 126:  Boy's tailor made fitted jacket. Black. Size 9-10. £12.99. Ref no. 23659865

Code 127:  Boy's tailor made fitted jacket. Brown. Size 9-10. £12.99. Ref no. 3698563

Code 128:  Hand-stitched chequered jumper. Blue/Black. Size M. £18.99. Ref no. 45698536

Code 129:  Men's skinny jeans. Black. Size 32 waist. £25.99. Ref no. 45236635

Code 130:  Men's skinny jeans. Navy. Size 34 waist. £25.99. Ref no. 41255325

Code 131:  Stallion t-shirt. White/Navy. Size M. £10.99. Ref no. 12696363

Code 132:  Prowler t-shirt. White/Black. Size S. £8.99. Ref no. 43696589

Code 133:  Woolly round neck jumper. Burgundy. Size M. £10.99. Ref no.  63569853

### Complete the missing entries for this customers order form

| Item no: | Product: | Colour: | Size: | Price: | Ref no: |
|---|---|---|---|---|---|
|  | Boy's tailor made fitted jacket |  | 9-10 |  | 3698563 |
| 126 |  | Black | 9-10 |  |  |
|  |  |  | M | £18.99 | 45698536 |
| 133 |  | Burgundy |  | £10.99 | 63569853 |
|  |  | Navy | Size 34 waist |  | 41255325 |

## INFORMATION HANDLING TEST EXERCISE 10

Study the information in the list below. The following is an extract from catalogue items for a carpet store.

### Catalogue items for a carpet store

Item 120:  Extra comfort and padded carpet. Black/Silver. Size 12x4. £29.99. Delivery date: 13/05/2014

Item 121:  Leopard print rug. Leopard print. Size 3x4. £16.99. Delivery date: 10/05/2014

Item 122:  Extra fitted carpet and skirting. Burgundy. Size 25x20. £38.99 Delivery date: 17/05/2014

Item 123:  Persian rug. Black. Size 10x8. £16.99. Delivery date: 21/05/2014

Item 124:  Persian rug. Brown. Size 12x8. £22.99. Delivery date: 22/05/2014

Item 125:  Extra comfort and padded carpet. Cream. Size 20x16. £46.99. Delivery date: 12/05/2014

Item 126:  Leopard print rug. Leopard print. Size 10x8. £32.99. Delivery date: 10/05/2014

Item 127:  Extra fitted carpet, skirting and underlay. Size 8x5. £120.00. Delivery date: 12/05/2014

### Complete the missing entries for this customers order list

| Item no: | Product: | Colour: | Size: | Price: | Delivery date: |
|---|---|---|---|---|---|
|  | Extra comfort and padded carpet |  | Size 12x4 |  | 13/05/2014 |
| 122 |  | Burgundy | Size 25x20 |  |  |
|  | Persian rug | Black |  | £16.99 |  |
|  |  | Brown | Size 12x8 | £22.99 |  |

## ANSWERS TO INFORMATION HANDLING INTERMEDIATE (SECTION 2)

## ANSWERS TO INFORMATION HANDLING TEST EXERCISE 1

| Entry Code | Price | Title | Author | Binding | ISBN |
|---|---|---|---|---|---|
| 127 | £26.99 | Youth and subcultures | Lewis, T | Hardback | 0-9647-2535 |
| 130 | £15.50 | Theories of Youth Culture | Davidson, H | Hardback | 0-7693-3586 |
| 131 | £12.99 | Understanding Contemporary Youth | Michaels, D | Hardback | 0-3635-6521 |
| 123 | £24.99 | Youth Studies | Blackman, R | Paperback | 0-3658-4532 |
| 124 | £18.99 | Introduction to Youth Culture | Downey, T | [download] | 0-4698-6983 |

## ANSWERS TO INFORMATION HANDLING TEST EXERCISE 2

| Code | Name | Colour | Size | Price | Ref No. |
|---|---|---|---|---|---|
| Code 110 | Sophie May backless dress | White/black | 10 | £45 | 2569873 |
| Code 112 | Summer backless prom dress | Aqua | 12 | £20.00 | 4258793 |
| Code 114 | Rosie Jane bodycon dress | Pink | 10 | £10 | 7456325 |
| Code 117 | Tailor made strapless dress | Black | 10 | £9.99 | 1236852 |
| Code 118 | Juliette Swirl bodycon dress | Green | 12 | £12.99 | 9635423 |

## ANSWERS TO INFORMATION HANDLING TEST EXERCISE 3

| Item no. | Product | Colour | Price | Ref no. | Page |
|---|---|---|---|---|---|
| 16 | Black mascara | Black | £5.99 | 14563259 | 5 |
| 25 | Shine and Clear Powder | Translucent | £3.99 | 56985326 | 9 |
| 20 | Shimmery Lip gloss | Pink | £3.99 | 45339522 | 7 |
| 25 | Shimmery Lip gloss | Clear | £3.99 | 45339523 | 7 |
| 40 | Shimmery Royal Blue eye palette | Royal blue | £10.99 | 78936234 | 14 |

## ANSWERS TO INFORMATION HANDLING TEST EXERCISE 4

| Item no: | Name on boots: | Boots: | Size: | Code: | Colour: | Right/Left/ Both boots: | Price: |
|---|---|---|---|---|---|---|---|
| 4 | D.P | Stallion Cutlass | 9 | 469256-15-650 | Black | both | £8 |
| 3 | White | Stallion Promptus | 8 | 698564-07456 | White | both | £20 |
| 5 | Lewis | Stallion Azrael | 10 | 259873-07-456 | White | Right boot | £10 |
| 7 | T.J. | Stallion Promptus | 10 | 698564-15-450 | White | both | £8 |
| 8 | JG8 | Prowler Nimbus | 7 | 659846-03-452 | Blue | both | £12 |

## ANSWERS TO INFORMATION HANDLING TEST EXERCISE 5

| Item no. | Team: | Premiership/ England: | Home/ Away: | Code: | Colour: | Straight/ Curved | Name printed: | Age printed: |
|---|---|---|---|---|---|---|---|---|
| 2 | England | England | Away | 65987245 | Navy | Straight | Jamie | 4 |
| 3 | North Ficshire | Premiership | - | 45698523 | Navy | Curved | Marianne | 10 |
| 5 | South Ficshire | Premiership | - | 25697523 | White | Straight | Big Daddy | 50 |
| 7 | England | England | Home | 46872587 | White | Straight | Elizabeth | 21 |
| 4 | England | England | Home | 65987426 | White | Curved | Madison | 12 |

## ANSWERS TO INFORMATION HANDLING TEST EXERCISE 6

| Code: | Title: | Author: | Copy: | Publisher: | Location: | Price: | ISBN: |
|---|---|---|---|---|---|---|---|
| 264 | An introduction to safety in the workplace | Harrison, A | Paperback | Graves | New York | £35.99 | 0-7896-4236 |
| 265 | Safety in action | Friend, J | Hardcopy | JJPB Books | London | £30.00 | 0-4526-8523 |
| 268 | Health procedures and safety guidelines | Richards, E | Hardcopy | JJPB Books | London | £16.99 | 0-1285-6539 |
| 270 | Guidelines for your workplace | Powley, D | Hardcopy | New Paper Books | London | £24.99 | 0-3596-0056 |
| 271 | The Workplace: Rules and Regulations | Ericson, P | Paperback | Graves | New York | £16.99 | 0-0069-5690 |

# ANSWERS TO INFORMATION HANDLING TEST EXERCISE 7

| Item no: | Product: | Colour: | Size: | Was: | Now: | Order no. |
|---|---|---|---|---|---|---|
| 12 | Camilla Red sequinned skirt | Red/Black | 12 | £30.00 | £15.00 | 4985232 |
| 14 | Lilly flowered white halter neck top | White/Flowery | 10 | £30.00 | £12.00 | 4569852 |
| 15 | Roxy May Gold flare skirt | Gold/Black | 12 | £50.00 | £20.00 | 9635891 |
| 17 | Phoebe Rose Prom Dress | Blue | 8 | £90.00 | £45.00 | 6596325 |
| 13 | Cassandra Black fitted dress | Black | 8 | £65.00 | £45.00 | 9635875 |

# ANSWERS TO INFORMATION HANDLING TEST EXERCISE 8

| Item no: | DVD/ Blu-ray | Film title: | Director: | Price: | Ref no: |
|---|---|---|---|---|---|
| 160 | Blu-ray | The Gremlin in the Grotto | Mickey Cohen | £12.99 | 5968759 |
| 161 | DVD | The Gremlin in the Grotto | Mickey Cohen | £9.99 | 2366984 |
| 163 | DVD | The Last Titan | Jennifer Grant | £8.99 | 4698677 |
| 166 | Blu-ray | War Without End | John Taylor | £15.99 | 6986326 |

## ANSWERS TO INFORMATION HANDLING TEST EXERCISE 9

| Item no: | Product: | Colour: | Size: | Price: | Ref no: |
| --- | --- | --- | --- | --- | --- |
| 127 | Boy's tailor made fitted jacket | Brown | 9-10 | £12.99 | 3698563 |
| 126 | Boy's tailor made fitted jacket | Black | 9-10 | £12.99 | 23659865 |
| 128 | Hand-stitched chequered jumper | Blue/Black | M | £18.99 | 45698536 |
| 133 | Woolly round neck jumper | Burgundy | M | £10.99 | 63569853 |
| 130 | Men's skinny jeans | Navy | Size 34 waist | £25.99 | 41255325 |

## ANSWERS TO INFORMATION HANDLING TEST EXERCISE 10

| Item no: | Product: | Colour: | Size: | Price: | Delivery date: |
| --- | --- | --- | --- | --- | --- |
| 120 | Extra comfort and padded carpet | Black/Silver | Size 12x4 | £29.99 | 13/05/2014 |
| 122 | Extra fitted carpet and skirting | Burgundy | Size 25x20 | £38.99 | 17/05/2014 |
| 123 | Persian rug | Black | Size 10x8 | £16.99 | 21/05/2014 |
| 124 | Persian rug | Brown | Size 12x8 | £22.99 | 22/05/2014 |

# ADVANCED
## SECTION 1

### PLEASE NOTE:

For this section, the questions are NOT an exact replica of the questions in your Scottish Police exam. Instead, they can be used to better your understanding and skills in regards to handling information.

*Study the following table and answer questions 1 to 5.*

*Based on 100 students and their marks in English, Maths and Science examinations.*

| Marks out of 40 | | | | |
|---|---|---|---|---|
| Subject | 30 and above | 20 and above | 10 and above | 0 and above |
| English | 19 | 52 | 91 | 100 |
| Maths | 13 | 36 | 90 | 100 |
| Science | 11 | 42 | 87 | 100 |
| AVERAGE | 11 | 43 | 89 | 100 |

## Question 1

The headmaster of the school, David, is examining the results. He has received a letter from a university, offering students a place on a mathematics graduate scheme. The letter informs David that only students who have received a pass mark of at least 50% can be offered a place on the course, provided they impress at an initial interview. Based on the results, how many students in Maths can apply for the graduate scheme?

| A | B | C | D | E |
|---|---|---|---|---|
| 49 | 13 | 36 | 19 | 27 |

## Question 2

Mr Irving, who is the head of the English department, has decided to run an after school English club, for students who are aged 12 and under. He needs to choose a selection from volunteers from the older year groups, who have taken their final English exam, to assist him in this endeavour. Mr Irving does not want any students who received lower than 50% in their final English examination to assist him. What percentage of students does he have available to him for assistance?

| A | B | C | D | E |
|---|---|---|---|---|
| 36% | 41% | 56% | 52% | 48% |

## Question 3

What is the difference between the number of students who achieved 30 or above in English and the number of students who achieved 20 and above in Science?

| A | B | C | D | E |
|---|---|---|---|---|
| 23 | 25 | 27 | 31 | 19 |

## Question 4

How many people scored 10 or above but below 20, in their Maths exam?

| A | B | C | D | E |
|---|---|---|---|---|
| 43 | 57 | 90 | 13 | 54 |

## Question 5

What subject had the highest number of students who scored below 10?

| A | B | C | D | E |
|---|---|---|---|---|
| English | Maths | Science | All the same | English and Maths |

*Study the following table and answer the questions 6 to 10.*

Employees in departments of a company

| Department | January | February | March | April | May | June |
|---|---|---|---|---|---|---|
| Marketing | 21 | 24 | 17 | 15 | 23 | 27 |
| Admin | 18 | 11 | 15 | 13 | 13 | 18 |
| Sales | 21 | 22 | 29 | 31 | 28 | 24 |
| IT | 19 | 13 | 17 | 18 | 22 | 25 |

## Question 6

The head of the company is conducting his yearly survey, of important business statistics, such as staff turnover, terminations, department employment rates and sick days. He has requested that his secretary supply him with the number of employees present within the company, in all of the available months excluding January, February, March, April and June. His secretary sends him a single number in response. What is this number?

| A | B | C | D | E |
|---|---|---|---|---|
| 71 | 78 | 83 | 86 | 89 |

## Question 7

After it was discovered that he had been embezzling funds, the previous head of the company has been arrested. The company is now under the leadership of a new owner – Mrs Dewford. Mrs Dewford wants her secretary to calculate the average number of employees for every single month, and then send her the results for February specifically. The secretary complies with this request, before emailing Mrs Dewford back the result – who then enters this into her spreadsheet. What number does Mrs Dewford enter into her spreadsheet?

| A | B | C | D | E |
|---|---|---|---|---|
| 9.75 | 17.5 | 11.5 | 13 | 19.75 |

## Question 8

Mrs Dewford's secretary seems to have jumbled up her results, and now the averages have been entered wrongly into the spreadsheet. To amend this, Mrs Dewford starts to work out the results herself. She correctly calculates the average number of employees, across the entire 6-month period, for Marketing, Sales and IT. What is the average number of the employees who have yet to be accounted for, in Mrs Dewford's table? Round your answer to the nearest whole number.

| A | B | C | D | E |
|---|---|---|---|---|
| 11 | 17 | 15 | 21 | 24 |

## Question 9

What was the largest number of people employed at one given time? (I.e. in any month, in any department).

| A | B | C | D | E |
|---|---|---|---|---|
| 29 | 31 | 27 | 35 | 26 |

## Question 10

What is the difference between the total number of employees in Marketing, and the total number of employees in Sales, across the six month period?

| A | B | C | D | E |
|---|---|---|---|---|
| 21 | 26 | 31 | 28 | 35 |

*Study the following chart and answer the questions 11 to 15.*

*A pie chart representing the number of crimes in a one month period.*

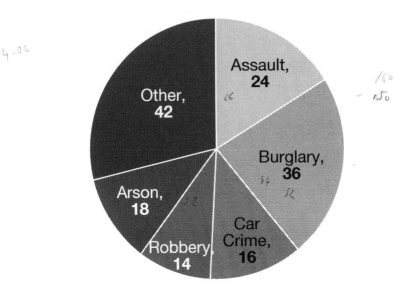

## Question 11

As part of an investigation into locally committed crimes, Detective Inspector Marsdan has asked his admin assistant to produce the above pie chart. Together, they work out that arson accounts for 12% of all crimes committed, with crimes that are not categorised – listed as other – at 28%. Based on these figures, what percentage of the crimes committed were assault based offences?

| A | B | C | D | E |
|---|---|---|---|---|
| 9% | 36% | 16% | 6% | 13% |

## Question 12

Assuming that arson accounts for 12% of all crimes committed, and crimes that aren't categorised count for 28%, work out the total number of offences that have been committed over the measurable period.

| A | B | C | D | E |
|---|---|---|---|---|
| 95 | 100 | 125 | 150 | 175 |

## Question 13

What was the average number of crimes across the one month period?

| A | B | C | D | E |
|---|---|---|---|---|
| 25 | 50 | 15 | 20 | 45 |

## Question 14

Inspector Marsdan is due to have a meeting with a government official, about crime rates in the local area. He is hoping that the findings displayed within the pie chart will convince the government to lend extra funding to his station, to help reduce crime. In order to do this, he needs to show the government official that there is a significant numerical leap between the number of the most dangerous crimes being committed, and the number of petty crimes. The official has emailed him in advance, asking him to make ready the differential between the most common and least common types of offence. What is this figure?

| A | B | C | D | E |
|---|---|---|---|---|
| 21 | 28 | 32 | 16 | 26 |

## Question 15

What percentage of the total number of crimes were burglary and arson-related?

| A | B | C | D | E |
|---|---|---|---|---|
| 21% | 55% | 61% | 42% | 36% |

*Study the following table and answer the questions 16 to 20.*

*BMW sales*

| Country | Jan | Feb | Mar | April | May | June | Total |
|---------|-----|-----|-----|-------|-----|------|-------|
| UK | 21 | 28 | 15 | 35 | 31 | 20 | 150 |
| Germany | 45 | 48 | 52 | 36 | 41 | 40 | 262 |
| France | 32 | 36 | 33 | 28 | 20 | 31 | 180 |
| Brazil | 42 | 41 | 37 | 32 | 35 | 28 | 215 |
| Spain | 22 | 26 | 17 | 30 | 24 | 22 | 141 |
| Italy | 33 | 35 | 38 | 28 | 29 | 38 | 201 |
| Total | 195 | 214 | 192 | 189 | 180 | 179 | 1149 |

The above table shows the sales across 6 countries for the model BMW for a 6 month period. The BMWs are imported to each country from a main dealer.

## Question 16

What percentage of the overall total was sold in April?

| A | B | C | D | E |
|---|---|---|---|---|
| 17.8% | 17.2% | 18.9% | 16.4% | 21.6% |

## Question 17

What percentage of the overall total sales were sold to the French importer?

| A | B | C | D | E |
|---|---|---|---|---|
| 15.6% | 18.2% | 18.9% | 25.6% | 24.5% |

## Question 18

What percentage of total imports is accounted for by the two smallest importers?

| A | B | C | D | E |
|---|---|---|---|---|
| 35.6% | 25.3% | 22.6% | 28.1% | 29.1% |

## Question 19

What is the average number of units per month imported to Brazil over the first 4 months of the year?

| A | B | C | D | E |
|---|---|---|---|---|
| 28 | 24 | 32 | 38 | 40 |

## Question 20

What month saw the biggest increase in total sales from the previous month?

| A | B | C | D | E |
|---|---|---|---|---|
| January | February | March | April | May |

**ANSWERS TO INFORMATION HANDLING ADVANCED (SECTION 1)**

**Q1. C = 36**

EXPLANATION = 50% of 40 = 20. Number of students who scored 20 and above in Maths = 36.

**Q2. D = 52%**

EXPLANATION = 100 students, 52 students achieved marks of 20 or above = 52%.

**Q3. A = 23**

EXPLANATION = Number of students with 30 or above in English = 19. Students with 20 or above in Science = 42. So 42 - 19 = 23.

**Q4. E = 54**

EXPLANATION = looking at the Maths row, you need to work out how many people scored 10 or above (90) but below 20. 36 of the 90 people scored 20 or above, therefore the number of people who scored 10 or above but below 20 is = 90 – 36 = 54.

**Q5. C = Science**

EXPLANATION = scores of 10 or below = English = 9, Maths = 10, Science = 13.

**Q6. D = 86**

EXPLANATION = 23 + 13 + 28 + 22 = 86.

**Q7. B = 17.5**

EXPLANATION = 24 + 11 + 22 + 13 = 70

70 ÷ 4 = 17.5.

**Q8. C = 15**

EXPLANATION = 18 + 11 + 15 + 13 + 13 + 18 = 88

88 ÷ 6 = 14.6. To the nearest whole number = 15.

**Q9. B = 31**

EXPLANATION = the largest number of people employed at any given time occurred in April, and that was for the department of Sales.

**Q10. D = 28**

EXPLANATION = Marketing 21 + 24 + 17 + 15 + 23 + 27 = 127.

Sales 21 + 22 + 29 + 31 + 28 + 24 = 155.

155 − 127 = 28.

**Q11. C = 16%**

EXPLANATION = 24 ÷ 150 x 100 = 16%.

**Q12. D = 150**

EXPLANATION = 42 + 18 + 14 + 16 + 36 + 24 = 150.

**Q13. A = 25**

EXPLANATION = 150 ÷ 6 = 25.

**Q14. B = 28**

EXPLANATION = 42 − 14 = 28.

**Q15. E = 36%**

EXPLANATION = 36 + 18 = 54

54 ÷ 150 x 100 = 36%.

**Q16. D = 16.4%**

EXPLANATION = to work out the percentage overall total that was sold in April, divide how many BMWs were sold in April (189) by the total (1149) and then multiply it by 100. (189 ÷ 1149 x 100 = 16.4%).

**Q17. A = 15.6%**

EXPLANATION = to work out the percentage overall total that was sold to France, divide how many BMWs were sold to France (180) by the total (1149) and then multiply it by 100. (180 ÷ 1149 x 100 = 15.6%).

### Q18. B = 25.3%

EXPLANATION = to work out the percentage overall for imports accounted by the two smallest importers, divide how many BMWs were sold from the two smallest importers (UK and Spain = 150 + 141 = 291) by the total (1149) and then multiply it by 100. (291 ÷ 1149 x 100 = 25.3%).

### Q19. D = 38

EXPLANATION = to work out the average number of units per month imported to Brazil over the first 4 months of the year, you add up the first 4 amounts (Jan-April) and then divide it by how many numbers there are (4). So, (42 + 41 + 37 + 32 = 152 ÷ 4 = 38).

### Q20. B = February

EXPLANATION = to work out the biggest increase in total sales from the previous month, you work out the difference between the totals for each of the month. Between January and February, there was an increase by 19. None of the other months have a bigger increase and therefore February is the correct answer.

# ADVANCED
## SECTION 2

### PLEASE NOTE:

For this section, the questions are NOT an exact replica of the questions in your Scottish Police exam. Instead, they can be used to better your understanding and skills in regards to handling information.

*Study the below table and answer the questions 1 to 5.*

The table shows imports for three types of wood over a 6 month period.

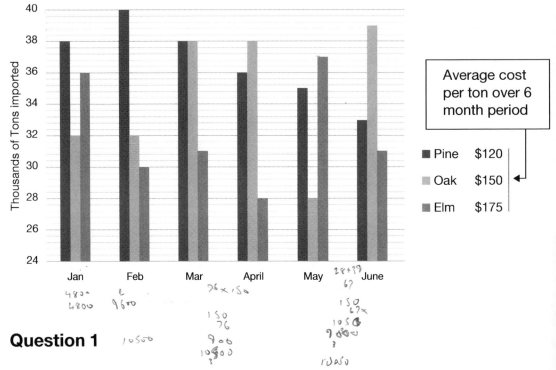

| Average cost per ton over 6 month period |
| --- |

■ Pine $120

▨ Oak $150

▦ Elm $175

## Question 1

What was the difference in thousands of tons between oak wood and elm wood imports in the first 3 months of the year?

| A | B | C | D | E |
| --- | --- | --- | --- | --- |
| 2,000 | 5,000 | 4,000 | 9,000 | 11,000 |

## Question 2

What was the total, in thousands of tons, for pine across the six month period?

| A | B | C | D | E |
| --- | --- | --- | --- | --- |
| 210,000 | 180,000 | 195,000 | 205,000 | 220,000 |

## Question 3

What was the total value of oak wood ($) imported over the 6 month period?

| A | B | C | D | E |
|---|---|---|---|---|
| 31,050 | 42,550 | 32,500 | 30,050 | 36,550 |

## Question 4

Which month showed the largest total decrease in imports over the previous month?

| A | B | C | D | E |
|---|---|---|---|---|
| March | January | June | February | April |

## Question 5

What was the average of elm wood imported over the 6 month period?

| A | B | C | D | E |
|---|---|---|---|---|
| 33.1 | 32.2 | 35.5 | 31 | 40.5 |

*Study the following table and answer the questions 6 to 10.*

The table shows the number of English papers published by top UK universities over a six year period.

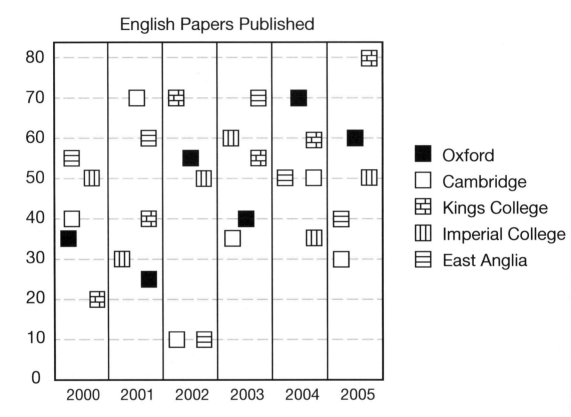

English Papers Published

Legend:
- ■ Oxford
- □ Cambridge
- ⊞ Kings College
- ⠿ Imperial College
- ⊟ East Anglia

## Question 6

How many papers did Oxford publish altogether?

| A | B | C | D | E |
|---|---|---|---|---|
| 275 | 215 | 325 | 285 | 260 |

## Question 7

Which college produces the closest number of total papers published, to the average number of papers published by all of the colleges over the total six years?

| A | B | C | D | E |
|---|---|---|---|---|
| Oxford | Cambridge | Kings College | Imperial College | East Anglia |

## Question 8

Which college showed the lowest differential, between its highest frequency publishing year and its lowest frequency publishing year?

| A | B | C | D | E |
|---|---|---|---|---|
| Oxford | Cambridge | Kings College | Imperial College | East Anglia |

## Question 9

Study the fluctuation patterns for each college, between years. Over the total of 6 years, which college contained the lowest total cumulative differential in yearly quantities of papers published?

For example: From 2000 to 2001, the number of papers published by Oxford decreased by 10 (-10). From 2001 to 2002, the number of papers published by Oxford increased by 30 (+30). From 2002 to 2003 the number of papers published by Oxford decreased by 15 (-15). From 2003 to 2004, the number of papers published by Oxford increased by 30 (+30). From 2004 to 2005, the number of papers published by Oxford decreased by 10 (-10).

So:

-10 + 30 – 15 + 30 – 10 = 25

| A | B | C | D | E |
|---|---|---|---|---|
| Oxford | Cambridge | Kings College | Imperial College | East Anglia |

## Question 10

How many papers were published by Cambridge University over the six year period?

| A | B | C | D | E |
|---|---|---|---|---|
| 275 | 285 | 235 | 245 | 280 |

*Study the following table and answer questions 11 to 15.*

Determine the correct code using the table provided. Orders are coded as follows: ORDER – COST – SHIPPING METHOD.

| ORDER | | COST | | SHIPPING METHOD | |
|---|---|---|---|---|---|
| Nails | 789 | Less than $100 | RR | Ultimate Delivery | 20 |
| Screws | 654 | $100-$250 | SS | International Parcel Delivery | 30 |
| Paint | 123 | $251-$350 | TT | Global Delivery Service | 40 |
| Saw | 912 | $351-$450 | UU | Lightning Express | 50 |
| Wood | 829 | $451-$550 | VV | Global Express | 60 |
| Telephone | 296 | $551-$650 | WW | Standard Mail | 70 |
| Clock | 328 | $651-$750 | XX | Customer Walk-In | 80 |

## Question 11

What would be the code for an order of paint that cost $120.75 and shipped by standard mail?

**A** – 789-TT-70

**B** – 829-SS-70

**C** – 123-SS-70
**D** – 123-SS-80

Answer

## Question 12

The code 829-UU-50 is CORRECT for an order of?

**A** – Wood costing $375.50 and shipped via Lightning Express
**B** – Paint costing $375.50 and shipped via Lightning Express
**C** – Wood costing $120.75 and shipped via airborne mail
**D** – Paint costing $375.25 and shipped via airborne mail

Answer

## Question 13

An order of screws arrived that cost $125.50. If the order is shipped via Global Delivery Service, what would it be coded?

**A** – 654-SS-40
**B** – 654-TT-40
**C** – 789-SS-40
**D** – 789-TT-50

Answer

## Question 14

An order of saws costing $514.25 shipped via International Parcel Delivery was coded 829-WW-30 in error. Of the following, which is the CORRECT code for this order?

**A** – 912-WW-30

**B** – 912-VV-30

**C** – 123-XX-50

**D** – 296-VV-40

Answer

## Question 15

An order of clocks costing $325.00 was sold to a walk-in customer. What is the CORRECT code for this transaction?

**A** – 296-RR-20

**B** – 654-RR-50

**C** – 328-SS-70

**D** – 328-TT-80

Answer

*Study the following table and answer the questions 16 to 20.*

Determine the correct training code based on the information provided in the table. Training instruction provided to employees is coded as: INSTRUCTOR – TRAINING – TRAINING SITE – DATE.

| INSTRUCTOR | CODE | TRAINING | CODE | TRAINING SITE | CODE | DATE | CODE |
|---|---|---|---|---|---|---|---|
| Walker | 222 | First Aid | H | Main Library | 353 | June 3 | AAA |
| Brown | 555 | Contracting | J | Ramsay Campus | 215 | June 4 | BBB |
| Powley | 777 | Budgeting | B | Arboretum | 795 | June 8 | CCC |
| Wells | 888 | Data Analysis | T | Powell Office | 635 | August 7 | DDD |
| White | 999 | Writing | I | Hyde Garage | 328 | August 11 | EEE |
| Thompson | 111 | Computers | N | Wester Hall | 701 | August 18 | FFF |
| Thomas | 333 | Mechanics | R | Public Works | 008 | August 23 | GGG |

## Question 16

The code 777-T-215-CCC is CORRECT for?

**A** – Contracting training taught by Thompson at the Main Library on August 7th

**B** – Contracting training taught by Powley at the Ramsay Campus on June 8th.

**C** – Data analysis training taught by Powley at the Ramsay Campus on June 8th.

**D** – Contracting training taught by Thomas at the Powell Office on August 18th.

Answer [                    ]

## Question 17

Walker wants to conduct writing training at the Powell Office. If the department schedules the training for the 23rd August, what would the code be?

**A** – 555-I-328-EEE

**B** – 222-I-635-GGG

**C** – 111-I-635-GGG

**D** – 111-T-795-DDD

Answer

## Question 18

Wells received her training schedule and saw the code 888-H-353-CCC. She notified her supervisor that the training needed to be moved to Wester Hall. The training was subsequently recoded to which of the following:

**A** – 888-H-701-CCC

**B** – 555-H-701-CCC

**C** – 999-B-701-AAA

**D** – 333-T-635-FFF

Answer

## Question 19

White was scheduled to conduct Mechanical training at Hyde Garage on June 4th, but Thomas had to substitute at the last minute. The revised code for the training is which of the following:

**A** – 333-J-795-CCC

**B** – 999-R-328-BBB

**C** – 333-R-328-BBB

**D** – 111-N-795-DDD

Answer

## Question 20

The code 555-B-353-FFF is CORRECT for?

**A** – Budgeting training taught by Brown at the Main Library on August 18th.

**B** – Contracting training taught by Wells at the Main Library on August 7th.

**C** – Budgeting training taught by Wells at the Main Library on August 7th.

**D** – Contracting training taught by Brown at the Main Library on August 18th.

Answer

*Study the following table and answer the questions 21 to 25.*

The following diagram shows the number of car accidents in the south east, UK.

| Year | Jan-Feb | Mar-April | May-Jun | July-Aug | Sept-Oct | Nov-Dec | Total |
|------|---------|-----------|---------|----------|----------|---------|-------|
| 2008 | 100 | 89 | 85 | 110 | 115 | 168 | 667 |
| 2009 | 179 | 165 | 154 | 120 | 169 | 184 | 971 |
| 2010 | 149 | 130 | 120 | 75 | 183 | 208 | 865 |
| 2011 | 168 | 142 | 135 | 102 | 128 | 147 | 822 |
| 2012 | 206 | 198 | 178 | 152 | 168 | 230 | 1132 |
| 2013 | 189 | 146 | 120 | 89 | 108 | 186 | 838 |
| Total | 991 | 870 | 792 | 648 | 871 | 1123 | 5295 |

## Question 21

What percentage of the total number of car accidents happened in Sept-Oct?

| A | B | C | D | E |
|---|---|---|---|---|
| 25 | 16.4 | 75 | 52.4 | 26.4 |

## Question 22

What is the average number of car accidents across the 12 month period for the year 2012?

| A | B | C | D | E |
|---|---|---|---|---|
| 94.3 | 92.8 | 188.6 | 175.5 | 160.3 |

## Question 23

What percentage of the monthly total was accounted for by the highest number of car accidents that occurred in Mar-April? Round your answer to one decimal place.

| A | B | C | D | E |
|---|---|---|---|---|
| 30 | 35.2 | 22.8 | 26.8 | 42.2 |

## Question 24

What percentage of the monthly total was accounted for by the lowest number of car accidents that occurred in Sept-Oct? Round your answer to the nearest whole number.

| A | B | C | D | E |
|---|---|---|---|---|
| 12 | 8 | 3 | 14 | 13 |

## Question 25

What is the difference between the year that had the lowest number of car accidents and the year that had the highest number of accidents?

| A | B | C | D | E |
|---|---|---|---|---|
| 462 | 465 | 468 | 463 | 464 |

*Study the following table and answer the questions 26 to 30.*

The following table shows the number of West End theatre tickets sold in a London theatre.

| Year | Jan-Feb | Mar-April | May-Jun | July-Aug | Sept-Oct | Nov-Dec | Total |
|------|---------|-----------|---------|----------|----------|---------|-------|
| 2008 | 210 | 315 | 345 | 165 | 268 | 167 | 1470 |
| 2009 | 570 | 562 | 763 | 719 | 589 | 345 | 3548 |
| 2010 | 596 | 587 | 526 | 358 | 687 | 348 | 3102 |
| 2011 | 458 | 324 | 459 | 763 | 359 | 368 | 2731 |
| 2012 | 358 | 361 | 206 | 586 | 236 | 695 | 2442 |
| 2013 | 359 | 354 | 469 | 454 | 462 | 523 | 2621 |
| Total | 2551 | 2503 | 2768 | 3045 | 2601 | 2446 | 15,914 |

## Question 26

What percentage of the overall total was the ticket rate between July-Aug?

| A | B | C | D | E |
|---|---|---|---|---|
| 15.2 | 19.1 | 22 | 31.5 | 35 |

## Question 27

What is average number of tickets sold per month in the 12 month period of 2012?

| A | B | C | D | E |
|---|---|---|---|---|
| 215.5 | 210.5 | 203.5 | 208.5 | 212.5 |

## Question 28

What is the total mean number of tickets sold in 2009 in the 12 month period?

| A | B | C | D | E |
|---|---|---|---|---|
| 295.7 | 285.7 | 265.7 | 210 | 125.7 |

## Question 29

What percentage of the total number of tickets sold is accounted for by the three years that sold the highest number of tickets in that year?

| A | B | C | D | E |
|---|---|---|---|---|
| 45 | 50.2 | 55.5 | 52.9 | 58.9 |

## Question 30

What percentage of total number of tickets sold is accounted for by the years 2013 and 2008?

| A | B | C | D | E |
|---|---|---|---|---|
| 28.7 | 25.3 | 28.3 | 25.7 | 30 |

*Study the following table and answer the questions 31 to 35.*

Determine the correct code using the table provided. Orders are coded as follows: ORDER – COST – SHIPPING METHOD.

| ORDER | CODE | COST | CODE | SHIPPING METHOD | CODE |
|---|---|---|---|---|---|
| Wardrobe | 008 | Less than $100 | AA | Ultimate Delivery | 00 |
| Bed Frame | 800 | $100-$250 | BB | International Parcel Delivery | 10 |
| Coffee Table | 456 | $251-$350 | CC | Global Delivery Service | 20 |
| Table and Chairs | 961 | $351-$450 | DD | Lightning Express | 30 |
| Sofa | 440 | $451-$550 | EE | Global Express | 40 |
| Mattress | 040 | $551-$650 | FF | Standard Mail | 50 |
| TV Unit | 222 | $651-$750 | GG | Customer Walk-In | 60 |

## Question 31

What would be the code for a wardrobe order that cost $356.00 and shipped by Lightning Express?

**A** – 800-DD-30

**B** – 008-DD-30

**C** – 008-CC-20

**D** – 800-FF-50

Answer [                    ]

## Question 32

The code 040-FF-40 is CORRECT for?

**A** – An order for a mattress costing $605 and shipped by Standard Mail.

**B** – An order for a mattress costing $210 and shipped by Global Express.

**C** – An order for a wardrobe costing $605 and shipped by Standard Mail.

**D** – An order for a mattress costing $605 and shipped by Global Express.

Answer

## Question 33

The code 440-BB-60 is CORRECT for an order of?

**A** – Sofa costing $180 and shipped via customer walk-in.

**B** – Sofa costing $180 and shipped via Global Delivery Service.

**C** – Sofa costing $300 and shipped via customer walk-in.

**D** – Sofa costing $251 and shipped via customer walk-in.

Answer

## Question 34

A customer orders a set of table and chairs costing $742 and shipped via International Parcel Delivery. What would the code be?

**A** – 440-EE-40

**B** – 222-GG-10

**C** – 961-GG-10

**D** – 800-DD-30

Answer

## Question 35

The code 456-EE-00 is CORRECT for an order of?

**A** – Coffee table costing $455 and shipped via Ultimate Delivery.

**B** – Coffee table costing $455 and shipped via Standard Mail.

**C** – Coffee table costing $250 and shipped via Ultimate Delivery.

**D** – Coffee table costing $455 and shipped via International Parcel Delivery

Answer

*Study the following table and answer the questions 36 - 40.*

The table shows the number of films released over a six year period. Use the information to answer the following questions.

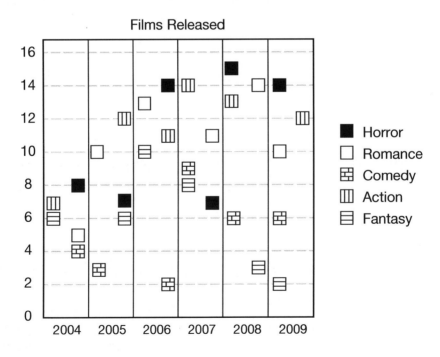

Films Released

## Question 36

In what year were the highest amount of Romance films released?

| A | B | C | D | E |
|---|---|---|---|---|
| 2004 | 2005 | 2006 | 2007 | 2008 |

## Question 37

How many Horror films were released across the six month period?

| A | B | C | D | E |
|---|---|---|---|---|
| 85 | 75 | 65 | 55 | 45 |

## Question 38

Which genre released the second highest number of films over the period?

| A | B | C | D | E |
|---|---|---|---|---|
| Horror | Romance | Comedy | Action | Fantasy |

## Question 39

How many films were released overall?

| A | B | C | D | E |
|---|---|---|---|---|
| 213 | 262 | 284 | 273 | 758 |

## Question 40

In what years did Romance films get released more than Horror films? Circle TWO.

| A | B | C | D | E |
|---|---|---|---|---|
| 2004 | 2005 | 2006 | 2007 | 2008 |

*Study the following table and answer the questions 41 - 45.*

Determine the correct code using the table provided. Orders are coded as follows: ORDER – COST – SHIPPING METHOD.

| ORDER | CODE | COST | CODE | SHIPPING METHOD | CODE |
|-------|------|------|------|-----------------|------|
| Windows | 368 | Less than $100 | DD | Ultimate Delivery | 30 |
| Doors | 147 | $100-$250 | EE | International Parcel Delivery | 40 |
| Paint | 123 | $251-$350 | FF | Global Delivery Service | 50 |
| Cupboards | 315 | $351-$450 | GG | Lightening Express | 60 |
| Tiles | 619 | $451-$550 | HH | Global Express | 70 |
| Sofa | 972 | $551-$650 | II | Standard Mail | 80 |
| Table and Chairs | 146 | $651-$750 | JJ | Customer Walk-In | 90 |

## Question 41

An order of doors arrived that cost $515.60. If the order is shipped via Lightning Express, it would be coded?

A – 619-II-50

B – 147-DD-90

C – 147-HH-60

D – 146-HH-70

Answer

## Question 42

The code 972-II-70 is CORRECT for an order of?

A – Sofa costing $275.50 and shipped via standard mail.

**B** – Tiles costing $558.99 and shipped via Global Express.

**C** – Sofa costing $558.99 and shipped via Global Express.

**D** – Cupboards costing $485.75 and shipped via Lightning Express.

Answer

## Question 43

What would be the code for an order of tiles that cost $325.60 and shipped by standard mail?

**A** – 619-FF-80

**B** – 315-GG-50

**C** – 315-FF-80

**D** – 146-DD-30

Answer

## Question 44

An order of doors costing $351.50 shipped via Ultimate Delivery was coded 315-DD-60 in error. Of the following, which is the CORRECT code for this order?

**A** – 146-GG-30

**B** – 147-GG-30

**C** – 972-EE-70

**D** – 619-JJ-80

Answer

## Question 45

An order of windows costing $720.90 was sold to a customer who requested it to be delivered by Lightning Express. What is the CORRECT code for this transaction?

**A** – 368-EE-50

**B** – 147-JJ-80

**C** – 368-JJ-60

**D** – 147-HH-60

Answer

*Study the following table and answer the questions 46 - 50.*

Determine the correct sports code based on the information provided in the table. Sports instructions provided to candidates is coded as: INSTRUCTOR - SPORT – SPORT SITE – DATE.

| INSTRUCTOR | CODE | SPORT | CODE | SPORT SITE | CODE | DATE | CODE |
|---|---|---|---|---|---|---|---|
| Johnson | 222 | Dance | C | Sports Centre | 367 | May 19th | DDD |
| Richards | 555 | Football | Y | Powell Hall | 645 | June 5th | AAA |
| Smith | 777 | Basketball | X | Anselm Hall | 125 | June 11th | BBB |
| Peters | 888 | Gymnastics | V | Augustine Hall | 463 | June 24th | CCC |
| Hampton | 444 | Tennis | E | Grove Green | 421 | August 7th | EEE |
| Grove | 111 | Hockey | T | Mote Park | 006 | August 9th | FFF |
| Perkins | 999 | Swimming | P | Mote Park Hall | 007 | August 24th | GGG |

## Question 46

Grove wants to conduct a Football lesson at the Sports Centre. If the centre schedules the lesson for the 9th August, the code would be?

**A** – 111-Y-367-FFF

**B** – 777-Y-367-FFF

**C** – 111-X-463-EEE

**D** – 111-V-125-CCC

Answer

## Question 47

The code 888-X-654-BBB is CORRECT for?

**A** – Football lesson taught be Peters at Powell Hall on June 11th.

**B** – Football lesson taught by Johnson at Grove Green on August 9th.

**C** – Basketball lesson taught by Peters at Powell Hall on June 11th.

**D** – Basketball lesson taught by Perkins at Augustine Hall on June 11th.

Answer

## Question 48

Smith received his schedule and saw the code 777-T-367-EEE. He notified his supervisor that the lesson needed to be moved to Mote Park. The training was subsequently recoded?

**A** – 777-T-006-FFF

**B** – 777-T-006-EEE

**C** – 777-T-007-EEE

**D** – 777-T-007-GGG

Answer

## Question 49

Richards was scheduled to conduct a Gymnastics lesson at Anselm Hall on June 5th, but Hampton had to substitute at the last minute. The revised code for the training is?

**A** – 444-C-654-DDD

**B** – 999-V-125-BBB

**C** – 444-V-125-AAA

**D** – 999-C-421-EEE

Answer

## Question 50

The code 555-E-367-DDD is CORRECT for?

**A** – Tennis lesson taught by Hampton at Grove Green on August 9th.

**B** – Tennis lesson taught by Hampton at Grove Green on June 24th.

**C** – Hockey lesson taught by Richards at the Sports Centre on May 19th.

**D** – Tennis lesson taught by Richards at the Sports Centre on May 19th.

Answer

## ANSWERS TO INFORMATION HANDLING ADVANCED (SECTION 2)

### Q1. B

EXPLANATION = to work out the difference, add up the first 3 months for Oak (32 + 32 + 38 = 102). Add up the first 3 months for Elm (36 + 30 + 31 = 97). So, the difference between Oak and Elm = 5 (thousands).

### Q2. E

EXPLANATION = 38 + 40 + 38 + 36 + 35 + 33 = 220 (220,000)

### Q3. A

EXPLANATION = 32 + 32 + 38 + 38 + 28 + 39 = 207 x 150 = 31,050.

### Q4. E

EXPLANATION = the highest decrease was between March and April, March's total = 107, April's total = 102. The difference is 5, no other months have a higher decreased number.

### Q5. B

EXPLANATION =193 ÷ 6 = 32.166. When rounded = 32.2

### Q6. D

EXPLANATION = the number of papers published by Oxford university, across the six month period = 35 + 25 + 55 + 40 + 70 + 60 = 285

### Q7. B

EXPLANATION = The average number of papers published by all of the colleges, over the six years, is 234. Cambridge has published 235 papers in total, making this the closest to the average.

### Q8. D

EXPLANATION = Imperial College's highest frequency publishing year was in 2003, where they published 60 papers. Imperial College's lowest frequency publishing year was in 2001, where they published 30 papers. This makes a differential of 30, which is the lowest of all of the colleges.

## Q9. E

EXPLANATION = East Anglia has the lowest total differential between years. From 2000 to 2001 the number of papers they published increased by 5 (+5). From 2001 to 2002 the number of papers they published decreased by 50 (-50). From 2002 to 2003 the number of papers they published increased by 60 (+60). From 2003 to 2004 the number of papers they published decreased by 20 (-20). From 2004 to 2005 the number of papers they published decreased by 10 (-10). This gives a total of -15.

## Q10. C

EXPLANATION = Overall, Cambridge University published 235 papers across the six year period.

## Q11. C

EXPLANATION = the correct answer is C. The code for paint (123) costing $120.75 (SS) and shipped by standard mail (70) is 123-SS-70.

## Q12. A

EXPLANATION = the correct answer is A. The code 829-UU-50 is correct for wood (829) costing $375.50 (UU) and shipped via Lightning Express (50).

## Q13. A

EXPLANATION = the correct answer is A. The entry would be coded as 654 (screws), SS (costing $125.50) and 40 (shipped via Global Delivery Service).

## Q14. B

EXPLANATION = the correct answer is B. The order should have been coded as 912 (saws), VV (costing $514.25), 30 (shipped via International Parcel Delivery).

## Q15. D

EXPLANATION = the correct answer is D. The most appropriate code for the transaction would be 328 (clocks), TT (costing $325) 80 (via customer walk-in).

## Q16. C

EXPLANATION = The correct answer is C. The code 777-T-215-CCC would signify that Powley (777) taught Data analysis Training (T) at the Ramsay Campus (215) on June 8$^{th}$ (CCC).

## Q17. B

EXPLANATION = The correct answer is B. The code for this training would be 222 (Walker) –I (Writing) –635 (Powell Office) –GGG (August 23$^{rd}$).

## Q18. A

EXPLANATION = The correct answer is A. The training would be recoded as 888 (Wells) –H (First Aid) –701 (Wester Hall) –CCC (June 8$^{th}$).

## Q19. C

EXPLANATION = The correct answer is C. The revised code for the training would be 333 (Thomas) –R (Mechanics) –328 (Hyde Garage) –BBB (June 4$^{th}$).

## Q20. A

EXPLANATION = The correct answer is A. This code is correct for Budgeting training (B) conducted by Brown (555) at the Main Library (353) on August 18$^{th}$ (FFF).

## Q21. B

EXPLANATION: to work out the percentage of the total number of car accidents that happened Sept-Oct, divide the number of car accidents that happened in Sept-Oct (871) by the total number of car accidents (5295) and then multiply it by 100. So, (871 / 5295 x 100 = 16.44).

## Q22. A

EXPLANATION: to work out the average number of car accidents across the 12 month period for the year 2012, divide the number of car accidents that happened in 2012 (1132) by the number of months (12) (Note: you would divide by 12 months and not 6, as the question asks for the average across '12' months) So, (1132 / 12 = 94.3).

## Q23. C

EXPLANATION: to work out the percentage of the monthly total that was accounted for by the highest number of car accidents that occurred in Mar-April, take the highest number of car accidents that happened in Mar-April

(198) and divide it by the monthly total (870) and multiply it by 100. So, (198 / 870 x 100 = 22.75) Rounded up to 1 decimal place = 22.8.

### Q24. A

EXPLANATION: to work out the percentage of the monthly total that was accounted for by the lowest number of car accidents that occurred in Sept-Oct, you divide the lowest number of car accidents that happened in Sept-October by the monthly total.

So, 108/871 = 12.3. Rounded to the nearest whole = 12.

### Q25. B

EXPLANATION = All you have to do is minus the lowest monthly total, 667, from the highest monthly total, 1132. This gives you 465.

### Q26. B

EXPLANATION: to work out the percentage of the overall total of tickets that was between July-Aug, divide the number of tickets sold in July-Aug (3045) by the overall total (15,914) and multiply it by 100. So, (3045 / 15,914 x 100 = 19.13) Rounded up to 1 decimal place = 19.1.

### Q27. C

EXPLANATION: to work out the average number of tickets sold per month over the 12 month period of 2012, you divide the total number of tickets sold in 2012 (2442) by the number of months (12). So, (2442 / 12 = 203.5).

### Q28. A

EXPLANATION: to work out the total mean number of tickets sold in the 12 month period of 2009, divide the total number of tickets sold in 2009 (3548) and divide it by the number of months (12). So, (3548 / 12 = 295.66) Rounded up to 1 decimal place = 295.7.

### Q29. E

EXPLANATION: to work out the percentage of the total number of tickets that is accounted for by the three highest years of sold tickets, add up the three highest years (2009, 2010, and 2011 = 3548 + 3102 + 2731 = 9381) and then divide it by the overall total (15,914) and multiply it by 100. So, (9381/ 15,914 x 100 = 58.94). Rounded up to 1 decimal place = 58.9.

**Q30. D**

EXPLANATION: to work out the percentage of the total number of tickets sold in 2008 and 2013, divide the number of tickets sold in 2008 and 2013 (1470 + 2621 = 4091) by the overall total (15,914) and then multiply it by 100. So, (4091 / 15,914 x 100 = 25.70).

**Q31. B**

EXPLANATION = The correct answer is B. The code for this order would be 008 (Wardrobe) –DD ($356) –30 (Lightning Express).

**Q32. D**

EXPLANATION = the correct answer is D. The code for mattress (040) costing $605 (FF) and shipped by Global Express (40).

**Q33. A**

EXPLANATION = the correct answer is A. The code for sofa (440) costing $180 (BB) and shipped by customer walk-in (60).

**Q34. C**

EXPLANATION = The correct answer is C. The code for this order would be 961 (Table and Chairs) –GG ($742) –10 (International Parcel Delivery).

**Q35. A**

EXPLANATION = The correct answer is A. The code for this order would be 456 (Coffee Table) –EE ($455) – 00 (Ultimate Delivery).

**Q36. E**

**Q37. C**

**Q38. A**

**Q39. B**

**Q40. B and D**

**Q41. C**

EXPLANATION = the correct answer is C. The entry would be coded as 147 (doors), HH (costing $515.60) and 60 (shipped via Lightning Express).

## Q42. C

EXPLANATION = the correct answer is C. The code 972-II-70 is correct for sofa (972) costing $558.99 (II) and shipped via Global Express (70).

## Q43. A

EXPLANATION = the correct answer is A. The code for tiles (619) costing $325.60 (FF) and shipped by standard mail (80).

## Q44. B

EXPLANATION = the correct answer is B. The order should have been coded as 147 (doors), GG (costing $351.50), 30 (shipped via Ultimate Delivery).

## Q45. C

EXPLANATION = the correct answer is C. The most appropriate code for the transaction would be 368 (windows), JJ (costing $720.90), 60 (via lightning express).

## Q46. A

EXPLANATION: The correct answer is A. The code for this lesson would be 111 (Grove) – Y (Football) –367 (Sports Centre) –FFF (August 9th).

## Q47. C

EXPLANATION: The correct answer is C. The code 888-X-654-BBB would signify that Peters (888) teaching Basketball (X) at the Powell Hall (654) on June 11th (BBB).

## Q48. B

EXPLANATION: The correct answer is B. The lesson would be recoded as 777 (Smith) –T (Hockey) –006 (Mote Park) –EEE (August 7th).

## Q49. C

EXPLANATION: The correct answer is C. The revised code for the training would be 444 (Hampton) –V (Gymnastics) –125 (Anselm Hall) –AAA (June 5th).

## Q50. D

EXPLANATION: The correct answer is D. This code is correct for a Tennis lesson (E) taught by Richards (555) at the Sports Centre (367) on May 19th (DDD).

# A Few Final Words...

## A FEW FINAL WORDS

You have now reached the end of the testing guide and no doubt you will be ready to take the Information Handling test element of the Scottish Police Test.

The majority of candidates who pass the police officer selection process have a number of common attributes. These are as follows:

### 1. They believe in themselves.

The first factor is self-belief. Regardless of what anyone tells you, you can become a police officer. Just like any job of this nature, you have to be prepared to work hard in order to be successful. Make sure you have the self-belief to pass the selection process and fill your mind with positive thoughts.

### 2. They prepare fully.

The second factor is preparation. Those people who achieve in life prepare fully for every eventuality and that is what you must do when you apply to become a police officer. Work very hard and especially concentrate on your weak areas.

### 3. They persevere.

Perseverance is a fantastic word. Everybody comes across obstacles or setbacks in their life, but it is what you do about those setbacks that is important. If you fail at something, then ask yourself '*why*' you have failed. This will allow you to improve for next time and if you keep improving and trying, success will eventually follow. Apply this same method of thinking when you apply to become a police officer.

### 4. They are self-motivated.

How much do you want this job? Do you want it, or do you *really* want it?

When you apply to join the police you should want it more than anything in the world. Your levels of self-motivation will shine through on your application and during your interview. For the weeks and months leading up to the police officer selection process, be motivated as best you can and always keep your fitness levels up as this will serve to increase your levels of motivation.

Work hard, stay focused, and secure your dream career!

*The how2become team*

The How2Become Team

P.S. Don't forget, you can get FREE access to more tests online at:

www.PsychometricTestsOnline.co.uk

# NEED A LITTLE EXTRA HELP WITH PASSING YOUR SCOTTISH POLICE ASSESSMENTS?

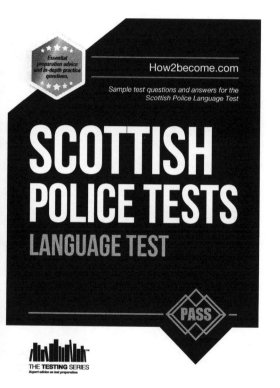

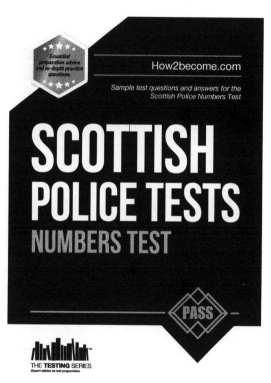

# FOR MORE INFORMATION ON OUR SCOTTISH POLICE GUIDES, PLEASE VISIT

# WWW.HOW2BECOME.COM

# Get Access To
# FREE
# Psychometric Tests

## www.PsychometricTestsOnline.co.uk

Printed in Great Britain
by Amazon

66138953R00068

# TEACHING
# GOD'S BIG STORY

Teaching God's Big Story
© Phil Crowter/The Good Book Company 2008. Reprinted 2010
(originally published as Preaching God's Big Story)

Published by
The Good Book Company Ltd
Elm House, 37 Elm Road
New Malden, Surrey KT3 3HB, UK
email: ppp@thegoodbook.co.uk

**Websites:**
**UK:** www.thegoodbook.co.uk
**N America:** www.thegoodbook.com
**Australia:** www.thegoodbook.com.au
**New Zealand:** www.thegoodbook.co.nz

ISBN: 9781906334574

Printed in India

# PLEASE READ THIS FIRST!

It is a very big honour to teach and preach God's words. Our prayer is that this book will help many teachers to do this well.

Paul says: "I have not held back from announcing to you the whole purpose of God" (Acts 20:27, GNB).

We find that only a few Christians understand how the Bible story fits together. They understand small parts, but not God's story from creation to Christ to the new creation. The talks in this book go through that wonderful story. They will help us to see how everything the Bible teaches fits together. This will make Christians stronger.

When we speak to people who are not yet Christians, we want to tell them about Jesus. But God wants people to understand many other things. *God's Big Story* picks out the main truths which God shows to us through the Bible. Encourage your friends and neighbours to hear these talks. Pray that many will believe as they see how the whole Bible is God's message to us.

*Teaching God's Big Story* is different from other PPP (*Pray Prepare Preach*) books. As well as the TALK pages, we give you EXTRA pages in colour. This will help you as teachers to see the whole Bible story better. The EXTRA pages will also give you important information about key Bible truths (like 'Satan' or 'the Tabernacle'). You may use some of this information in your talks, or you could use them in EXTRA studies with a smaller group.

[The back cover opens out to show eight pictures. These show how the main Bible events fit together. Use this in your talks. It will help your listeners to remember and follow God's Big Story. Show your listeners where you have got to in the Bible story.]

Before you begin to teach the first talk, please take time to look at:

A. How to prepare a talk
B. How to use *Teaching God's Big Story*
C. Introduction to the Bible story

*Phil Crowter*
*September 2008*

# Contents

A. How to prepare a talk . . . . . . . . . . . . . . . . . . . . . . . . . . . . . 5

B. How to use "Teaching God's Big Story" . . . . . . . . . . . . . . 6

C. Introduction to the Bible story . . . . . . . . . . . . . . . . . . . . 10

- Bible books

- God's big story

- The big story plan

- Plan for this book

- How to use this book

D. TALKS and EXTRA help/pages . . . . . . . . . . . . . . . . . . . . 18

**1. Pray for God's help.**

**2. Read the Bible section several times.**
Use ◙ **Background** to help you to understand the section.
Use ◉ **Notes** to help you to understand difficult Bible verses.

**3. Try to find the main point that God is teaching us in the Bible section.**
Use ⊙ **Main point** to help you.

**4. Pray for your people. Think how this Bible section will help them.**
Use ⊠ **Something to work on** to help you.

**5. Write your talk in your own language. Start with the main points which the Bible teaches.**
Use our notes in the **TALK** section to help you.

**6. Now write a beginning and an end for your talk.**

**7. Check what you have done.**

- Is the **main point** clear?
- Do you show them what the **Bible** teaches?
- Do you use **word pictures** to help your people understand and remember?
- Do you **connect** with the people?
- What do you hope will **change**?

**8. Pray that God will speak through your words. Pray that his truth will change people.**

*For more help read the next section.*

Every time you prepare a talk, begin with these things:

• Pray for God's help

• Read the Bible section

• Try to find the main point that God teaches us in the Bible section.

Then you can use these notes to help you. There are two pages for each talk. The first page helps you to think about the Bible section. The second page gives you headings and ideas for a talk.

When you see this symbol , you need to read what the Bible says.

## STUDY page:
*Understand the Bible*

The first page helps you to understand the Bible section.

⦿ **Background:** It is important to think about how the TALK section fits into the big story of the Bible.

The **Background** section will help you to do this.

Use this help in your talk. The EXTRA pages will give you more background help. Also use a large picture of the 8 main events. This will help your listeners to understand the big story.

⦿ **Main point:** We have put the most important point in a few words. Think about this point. Can you see this is what the Bible section is teaching? Try to make sure that this point is very clear in your talk.

✴ **Something to work on:** This section chooses something from the Bible section which you need to think about. It is important to work hard to understand the Bible. Think carefully about how to teach the point in this section.

⦿ **Notes:** This section tells you about difficult Bible verses. It will help you not to make mistakes when you are teaching.

# TALK page:
## *Teach the Bible*

The second page helps you to teach the Bible section. You must also do your own work. This page gives you ideas. You must take the ideas and use them in the best way. We give you the bones, but you must put the meat on the bones!

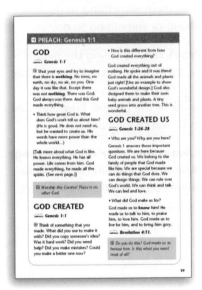

## 1. Things we have written to help you:

### • Two or three headings.

These are written **LIKE THIS**

These headings will help you to teach

the Bible clearly. You can change the headings to make them better for your people.

### • **We show you what the Bible says.**
We want people to listen to the Bible. In your talk, point people to what the **Bible** says. If they have a Bible, ask them to find the verse you are talking about. This symbol will help you know when to do this.

### • **We explain what the Bible is teaching.**
You need to think how to explain the Bible so that your people understand. You know your people. We do not know your people. Your words are better than our words.

### • **We sometimes use a word picture.**
Here is an example from the notes on Genesis 6:5-22.

⊕ *Show a piece of fruit. It has some bad spots on it. You may think that you can cut out the bad bits and eat the fruit. But this one is bad all the way through!*

This word picture may not be the best for your listeners. You may not have fruit like this. A Bible teacher must find a better word picture to help the people to understand.

You will need to find many more

word pictures to help teach the Bible truth. Be very careful that the word picture teaches what the Bible is saying.

- **We show you how to connect the Bible teaching to your people.**
  It is important to hear God's word speaking **to us**. We need to know how the Bible teaching changes us. Here is an example from Genesis 1:1:

> ⟫ *Worship this Creator!*
> *There is no other God.*

- **We give you one or two ideas.**
  You need to think of more ways to connect the Bible to your people. You know the people. You know how the Bible needs to change their lives.

## 2. Other things you will need to do:

- **Think how to start your talk.**
  Your people need to see why it is important to listen today. Tell them what you will teach them from the Bible. Tell them why it is important for them.

- **Think how to end your talk.**
  Remind them of the main points. Give them something to think about, or something to do.

- **Pray!** You are telling the people God's truth from God's word. Pray that God will use your words to speak to the people. Pray that God's truth will change people.

- **Always use your own language. Never** say things in English if the people do not speak English well.

# TEACHING
# GOD'S BIG STORY

(The different kinds of books and how they tell God's big story.)

### OLD TESTAMENT

### HISTORY

The first 5 books are called the LAW OF MOSES. They tell the story of creation... man's sin... the Exodus... wandering in the desert... to the border of the Promised Land.

Joshua to Esther tell the story of God's people in the **Promised Land**; their idol worship... their kings... punishment in foreign countries... return to the Promised Land.

### POETRY

Songs to praise God. Wise words to teach how to live. (Mostly written by King David or Solomon).

### PROPHETS

The prophets are God's messengers. Many of the prophets wrote in the time of the kings. They tell Israel to come back to God. They warn of God's punishment and promise God's special plans for the future.

Some prophets wrote later, when God's people were away in foreign lands, or when they returned home.

To understand any of the prophets we must know when each one wrote. We must know where the prophet fits in the HISTORY books.

### NEW TESTAMENT

### HISTORY

The four GOSPELS tell the good news about Jesus' life and death. This is what the Old Testament points to. Here is the answer to how man and God can be friends again.

### ACTS

Tells us about God's new family (the church), and how the good news about Jesus spread to many countries.

### PAUL'S LETTERS

(from Romans to Philemon).

Paul wrote most of his letters to help the new churches round the world. (Romans to Thessalonians)

Letters to Timothy and Titus encourage the pastors.

Philemon is a personal letter.

### OTHER LETTERS

Other apostles (Peter, James, John and Jude) wrote these. They wrote them to encourage churches in hard times.

We do not know who wrote Hebrews.

### REVELATION

This tells us John's visions. It shows in picture language that Jesus has won – over death, sin and Satan. God and his people will live as friends together in a wonderful land.

# GOD'S BIG STORY

There are different ways to think about the Bible. The diagram below is one way.

**The New Testament (New T)** fits on top of the Old T. It gives us the finished picture.

The **Old Testament (Old T)** is like a foundation or base. It tells us the things we need to know about God and about us. But the Old T is not enough on its own. It leads us to Jesus and the cross.

NEW TESTAMENT

OLD TESTAMENT

## Story line

Another way to look at the Bible is a **story line**. It follows the story of the Bible from beginning to end. This book will follow the story line of the Bible. Here is a simple picture of it.

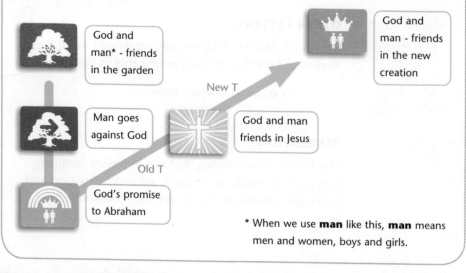

God and man* - friends in the garden

Man goes against God

New T

God and man friends in Jesus

God and man - friends in the new creation

Old T

God's promise to Abraham

* When we use **man** like this, **man** means men and women, boys and girls.

The Bible tells the story of how men and women went away from God. It tells us about God's plan to be friends with his people again.

One of the most important parts of the Bible is...

Promise

**God's promise to Abraham.**

God promises Abraham that he will make people friends with God again. God promises them a Home Land, where he will be with them and bless them.

In the **Old Testament**, God gives the people of Israel a promised land. But they always sin and spoil everything. God's promise to Abraham means much more than the Promised Land of Israel. The story of the people of Israel in the Promised Land teaches us more. It makes us look for a Saviour who will bring man back to God.

In the **New Testament**, God sends his Son, Jesus. On the cross, Jesus solves the sin problem that keeps us away from God. Now people from all round the world can be friends with God.

This is how God keeps his promise to Abraham. In the end, God will be special friends with his people for ever. There will be a new heaven and a new earth – a new Promised Land.

The next page tells the same story, but shows more detail.

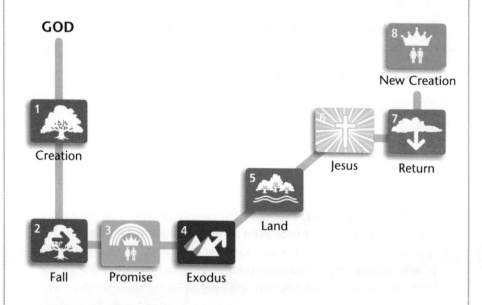

**GOD**

Creation

New Creation

Jesus

Return

Land

Fall

Promise

Exodus

This shows the eight main events in the Bible story.

It will be the plan that we follow through the book.

This shows how man goes away from God and how God brings his people back. See that **8. New Creation** is higher than **1. Creation**. This is to show that God brings us even closer to him than Adam and Eve were in the garden. The new creation (a new heaven and a new earth) is much better than the first creation was!

Creation

**God creates everything good.**

God creates the first people. He is friends with them in a beautiful garden.

Fall

**Man sins and now cannot be friends with God.**

Adam and Eve go against what God told them. The Bible calls this sin. Sin brings death into the world. Now man cannot be friends with God. God sends him away.

Promise

**God's special promise to Abraham.**

God promises Abraham that he will make people friends with God again. God promises them a Home Land, where he will be with them and bless them.

Exodus

**God rescues his people from Egypt.**

The people of Israel are from Abraham's family line. God says that they are his special people. They become slaves in Egypt. God rescues his people from Egypt. They travel to the Promised Land.

Land

**God blesses his people in the Promised Land.**

God brings his people into the Promised Land. They defeat the enemies. God blesses them. But they worship false gods. God gives them trouble from the nations round them. In the end, enemies take God's people away to foreign lands. They return, but they still sin. They need a Saviour to save them from their sin.

Jesus

**God sends Jesus to save people everywhere.**

Jesus comes to die on a cross and rise from the dead. This is the only answer for our sin. Now God and man can be friends again.

Return

**Jesus will return to end the world and judge everyone.**

People who follow Jesus are friends with God. But it is not easy to follow Jesus. The devil is against us. We look forward to the time when Jesus will come back. He will make everything right.

New Creation

**God's people will be perfect friends with God for ever.**

God will punish everyone who has not trusted Jesus. God will send them away from him for ever, to hell. God's people will live with him in the new heaven and new earth. They will love and serve Jesus for ever. God's promise will come true completely.

## PLAN FOR THIS BOOK

| **Main event** | **Talks** | **Extra** |
|---|---|---|

Creation

**1** God the Creator

Satan and Spirit World

Fall

**2** Man's sin and fall
**3** The Flood –
judgement and rescue

Promise

**4** Promise!

The story so far

Exodus

**5** Rescue – Saviour
**6** Rescue – Sacrifice
**7** Rescue – Enemy judged
**8** 10 Commandments
**9** Tabernacle – God with us
**10** Unbelief

Sacrifices in Old Testament
Exodus Map + Timeline
Old T laws + Tabernacle

Story so far + map

Land

**11** Promised Land
**12** False gods
**13** God's King!
**14** A song of trust
**15** Prophets - judgement + hope
**16** Return!

Story fill-in
Kings of Israel and Judah
Songs and wise sayings
Prophets
Story so far

Jesus

**17** Jesus – promised Saviour
**18** Jesus – came to die
**19** Jesus – risen
**20** Jesus' church
**21** A letter to encourage

Coming of the Holy Spirit
The good news goes out
Story so far + New T letters

Return

**22** Jesus' return
**23** Judgement Day

Revelation

New Creation

**24** Promise kept –
New Creation

Final summary

### 1. Talks

The TALKS show how the Bible tells God's story. Each TALK is about an important truth that God wants us to know.

Start at the beginning and teach one TALK each week. Then your listeners will start to understand God's wonderful story.

- This will be very important for **believers**. It will help them to see how the Bible fits together.

- It will also be important for people who are **not yet Christians**. These truths are what they need to know. It is God's story, which saves!

See how there are eight main Bible events, with eight pictures. This gives us the outline or bones of the story. For some of these (like CREATION) there is just one TALK. And for some Bible events (like EXODUS), there are many TALKS. This is because God has many different things for us to learn from these main events.

To help your people, draw a big picture to show the eight main events. Every week, remind them where you have got to on the picture.

### 2. Extra pages

The EXTRA pages are mostly to help **you**. They help you to get a better understanding of God's big story.

Sometimes you may want to teach your people these things too. Be careful not to give them too many facts to learn. It may confuse them.

Or, you may want to do EXTRA studies with a group of people who learn well. You could meet with them one day each week.

# GOD THE CREATOR

**1**

## ◉ Background

📖 *Genesis 1-2.* Many cultures have stories about how the world began. But Genesis 1-2 is different. God gives us the truth. Genesis 1-2 tells us what really happened.

📖 *John 1:1-3.* This shows us that Jesus ('the Word') was there in the beginning. Jesus is God. The Father created the world through Jesus (Colossians 1:15-17).

## ◉ Main point

God created the world.
God created us.

## ⊠ Things to work on

1. When we say 'God', what do people understand? Do they have their own ideas? In your country, are there many 'gods', or many ideas about God?

You may need to explain that God is different to all these ideas. He was there before the sea, mountains and trees! He was there before people made 'gods' from wood and stone. God was there before the spirits. God is someone who we can know. He made us like him in some ways (Genesis 1:27). This is so that we can know God.

2. Some Christians worry about how the Bible fits with science. The important thing is to believe what the **Bible** says. It tells us of a real Adam and Eve, the first people. They were not made from animals - they were made special, in God's image (like him). Science often changes, but God's word never changes! Often we find that science does agree with what the Bible says.

## ◉ Notes

**Genesis 1:2.** God is Father, Son and Holy Spirit. He is one God, but three persons. Genesis 1:26 does not say: 'Let me make man in my image.' God says: 'Let us make man in our image'.

**Genesis 1:26.** 'in our image'. This means 'like God'. This does not mean that we are the same as God. It means that we can think and talk, feel and love, as God does. Animals cannot do this!

**Genesis 1:26-28.** God told the man (and woman) to **rule over** his world. He made it and we must care for it. This does **not** mean men should fight to have power over each other. It does **not** mean that men should use their power to hurt women.

## → PREACH: Genesis 1:1

# GOD

📖 *Genesis 1:1*

⊕ Shut your eyes and try to imagine that there is **nothing**. No trees, no earth, no sky, no air, no you. One day it was like that. Except there was not **nothing**. There was God. God always was there. And this God made everything.

• Think how great God is. What does God's work tell us about him? (He is good. He does not need us, but he wanted to create us. His words have more power than the whole world…)

[Talk more about what God is like. He knows everything. He has all power. Life comes from him. God made everything; he made all the spirits. (See next page.)]

> ⊠ *Worship this Creator! There is no other God.*

# GOD CREATED

📖 *Genesis 1:1*

⊕ Think of something that you made. What did you use to make it with? Did you copy someone's idea? Was it hard work? Did you need help? Did you make mistakes? Could you make a better one now?

• How is this different from how God created everything?

God created everything out of nothing. He spoke and it was there! God made all the animals and plants just right! [Use an example to show God's wonderful design.] God also designed them to make their own baby animals and plants. A tiny seed grows into another tree. This is wonderful.

# GOD CREATED US

📖 *Genesis 1:26-28*

• Who are you? Why are you here?

Genesis 1 answers those important questions. We are here because God created us. We belong to the family of people that God made like him. We are special because we can do things that God does. We can design things. We can rule over God's world. We can think and talk. We can feel and love.

• What did God make us for?

God made us to **know** him! He made us to talk to him, to praise him, to love him. God made us to live for him, and to bring him glory. *In what ways do we worship?*

📖 *Revelation 4:11*

> ⊠ *Do you do this? God made us to honour him. Is this what you want most of all?*

✓ Craft – clay or similar?

19

## Where did the spirit world come from?

God created everything – he made it all perfect and good.

📖 **Genesis 1:31**

This includes the spirit world:

📖 **Colossians 1:15-16**

God was there before the spirits – He is the one who created them (even Satan and the evil spirits)!

God created the spirits for him – to serve him.

So why do we fear the spirits? They are only created beings.

We should fear only the Creator God – and worship only Him.

## Where did evil and Satan come from?

The Bible does not tell us clearly how evil came into the perfect world that God made. But some verses help us to understand:

📖 **Revelation 12:7-9.** This takes us back to the beginning.

There was a war in heaven. Some of the angels led by Satan chose to fight against God. They wanted to have God's place. They wanted to be boss.

That could never be! So God threw Satan and the bad angels out of heaven.

Remember, that many spirits – the angels – did not rebel against God. (They still serve God and his people.)

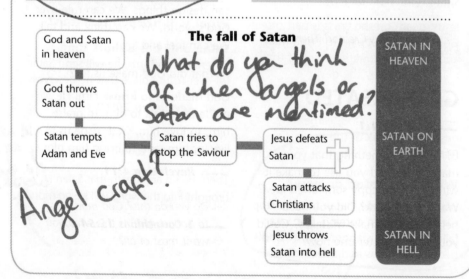

**The fall of Satan**

| | | | | |
|---|---|---|---|---|
| God and Satan in heaven | | | | SATAN IN HEAVEN |
| God throws Satan out | | | | |
| Satan tempts Adam and Eve | Satan tries to stop the Saviour | Jesus defeats Satan | | SATAN ON EARTH |
| | | Satan attacks Christians | | |
| | | Jesus throws Satan into hell | | SATAN IN HELL |

*What do you think of when angels or Satan are mentioned?*

*Angel craft?*

So God created Satan as an angel, but he and many other angels went against God. God threw them down to the world. Now Satan wanted to turn the man and woman away from God. Satan came to Eve in the garden as a snake and tempted her. He said that she and Adam could be like God.

## What success does Satan have?

**Satan has already lost.** No one can fight against God and win!

God promises what will happen in

 *Genesis 3:15*

A man who comes from Eve will crush (destroy) Satan's head. This is the first time that the Bible points forward to Jesus. On the cross, Jesus destroyed the enemy, Satan.

*Hebrews 2:14-15*

Jesus' death defeated the devil. Jesus sets believers free from the fear that Satan brings us.

Jesus' death on the cross is part of God's wonderful plan to bring man and God back together. Part of that plan is to destroy the devil.

*1 John 3:8*

Jesus, the Son of God, came to destroy the work of the devil. Praise him!

## What does Satan do now?

Before Jesus came, Satan tried to stop the Saviour from coming. But Satan failed. Now he is angry against God's people. He hates and attacks God's

### Satan's power is limited

- Satan can only do what God allows. God is always in control. This is clear from the story of Job (Job 2:1-10).

- Satan and the evil spirits can only be in one place at a time. They are not like God! They only know some things.

people. Satan does all he can to turn men and women against God.

You can see this spiritual battle clearly in the New Testament. Satan tries to hurt the church. He tempts Christians away from God.

Jesus gives his people the weapons for the fight. As we trust Jesus, **we can stand** against Satan.

*Ephesians 6:10-20*

## What will happen to Satan?

**Satan only has a short time.** When Jesus returns, he will send Satan for ever to the place that he deserves.

*Revelation 20:10*

We can look forward to that day. Jesus will send Satan to hell for ever.

Then the sin and death that Satan brought into the world will be no more.

*1 Corinthians 15:54-57*

'The enemy has been defeated' -song

STUDY: Genesis 3

# 2 MAN'S SIN AND FALL

## ◉ Background

God created everything out of nothing. It was all very good (Genesis 1:31). He made the man and woman to be like him. He talked with them in the wonderful Garden of Eden. Everything was perfect.

They had lovely fruit to eat, but they must not eat from one tree. This tree had a name – 'the tree that makes you know good and evil'.

### 📖 Genesis 2:15-16

(See EXTRA page on SATAN). The garden had an evil visitor. The devil, Satan, wanted to make Man go against God. The devil came as a snake. He began to talk to Eve...

### 📖 Genesis 3

## ◉ Main point

Man went against God. (We often call this 'the Fall of man'. Man 'fell' away from God.) He can no longer be God's friend. It spoiled God's perfect world.

## ✱ Something to work on

The first 'sin' shows what all sin is. Often, people think that sin is just something bad that they do. But sin is much more serious than that.

Adam and Eve ate the forbidden fruit. This was wrong, but their sin was more serious than that. **They went against God.** They wanted to please themselves, not God. They did not want God to tell them what to do.

We are Adam's children. We sin like him. Like Adam, we do not want God to rule over us. We want to live the way we want to. This is sin.

Think how best to explain this to your listeners.

## ◉ Notes

**Genesis 3:5.** The devil tempts Eve with bad ideas. 'God does not want the best for you. He wants the power for himself. You can be happy if you eat the fruit.'

**Genesis 3:15.** This is the first promise about Jesus. A special Man will come from Eve's family line. He will defeat the devil.

**Genesis 3:16.** Now husbands and wives will both want to be the boss. Husbands will be cruel. Wives will go against their husbands. This will make many problems.

**Genesis 3:17.** Sin has spoiled our **world**. This is the reason for floods and diseases and other problems.

Newspapers – what jumps out that is happening because of the fall

# THE SIN

📖 *Genesis 3:1-6*

Adam and Eve were our first parents. What they did in the Garden of Eden, they did for us all. This is not just an old story. This is **our** story. This is how we became evil. This is how we spoiled our world.

We cannot blame Adam and Eve for our sin. God blames **us**. We go against God in just the same way.

When the devil tempted Adam and Eve...

- What did they want? To please God – or to please themselves?

- Who did they trust? God, their Creator – or the devil?

They turned their backs on their God! It was that bad. God had given them everything to make them happy. But they wanted to take God's place and rule everything.

> ➢ This is our sin too. God is sad when we steal or lie or hate. But our real sin is worse than those things. Like Adam, we do not want God to rule over us. We want to live the way we want to. We want to please ourselves. This is **sin**.

# THE RESULTS

*actually do!*

⊞ Show an egg. What would happen if you dropped it on the floor?

It was like that when Adam and Eve first sinned. God's perfect world was spoiled. Now it was like that broken egg. Everything was broken. And, like an egg, it was impossible to mend.

- Sin made them hurt **themselves**. They were ashamed 📖 *Genesis 3:7.* But it was much more serious than that. They now will die (Genesis 2:17).

- Sin made them hurt **each other.** 📖 *Genesis 3:12, 16.* They began to blame each other, to quarrel. Sin spoiled their perfect friendship.

- Sin hurt **their world.** 📖 *Genesis 3:17-19*

- Worst of all, sin spoiled **their friendship with God.** 📖 *Genesis 3:10, 22-24.* God sent Adam and Eve away. They could not live with him. Sin separates us from God, for ever.

> ➢ Do you see now how bad your sin is? It is bad because it is against **God**. It is bad because it spoils everything. It keeps us away from God. It leads to death and hell. But this is not the end of the story! The Bible tells us God's plan to bring us back to him.

# 3 THE FLOOD – JUDGEMENT AND RESCUE

## ◉ Background

God made everything good. Man sinned and spoiled everything.

Things got worse. Hundreds of years went by, and people became full of evil.

### 📖 Genesis 6:5

God was very sad. He hated all the evil so much that he planned to judge the world. He planned to kill everyone in a flood. But he wanted to save Noah and his family. So he told Noah to build a boat ('ark').

### 📖 Genesis 6:5-22

## ◉ Main point

God must judge our evil lives. But he has a plan to save his people.

## ✴ Something to work on

It is very important that your listeners understand two things. Unless they see these things, they will not see that they need Jesus to save them!

**1. We are very bad.** We are not good, with bits of bad. We are bad all the way through, with bits of good! We are too bad to make ourselves better.

**2 We are in big trouble.** God will judge our evil lives. He sees how bad

we are. God will not send a flood. But worse, he will send us away from him for ever.

## ◉ Notes

**Genesis 6:5, 11.** See how completely evil man became. All our thoughts were evil. (This is because we do not want to please God. We only want to please ourselves.) We are bad all the way through. (We call this truth 'total depravity'.) This does not mean that we are as bad as we can be. There are still some good things left in everyone.

**Genesis 6:6-7.** God decided to kill ('wipe out') the people he made. God hates evil and he must judge us. But see how this hurts God. This is because God is love.

### 📖 2 Peter 3:3-10

**Genesis 6:7.** God was sorry that he made man. This shows how sad God is. It does not mean that God made a mistake! God knew what would happen. Even before Adam and Eve sinned, God's plan was to save us from our sin!

**Genesis 6:8-10.** Noah was not perfect! But God had changed his heart. So Noah wanted to please God.

(6)

# → PREACH: Genesis 6:5-22

## GOD JUDGES EVIL

### 📖 Genesis 6:5-6

⊞ Show a piece of fruit. It has some bad spots on it. You may think that you can cut out the bad bits and eat the fruit. But this one is bad all the way through!

We are like that fruit. We may not look too bad. But we are bad inside. Our thoughts are bad, because we do not love God. 📖 Genesis 6:5.

Do you think that everyone killed people? Did everyone lie and steal? No! Like us, many of them seemed nice people. But what does God say about them? 📖 Genesis 6:5-6. (People were no better **after** the flood; Genesis 8:21, Psalm 14:1-3.)

God's beautiful world pleased him a lot. But the people spoiled it. Now God was so sad. He had to judge the world. Everyone would die in a flood.

### 📖 Genesis 6:6, 12, 13

[Tell the story. Noah builds the ark for many years. He tells people that God will send a flood. But people will not listen to him. They laugh at him. Then the rain comes. The people drown. They die. They meet God their Judge.]

⟩⟩ God promises to judge the world again. Then Jesus will come back. We will all meet God, our Judge.

Most people just laugh. They think that there is plenty of time. But you need to be ready. Are you ready? (2 Peter 3:3-10)

## GOD RESCUES HIS PEOPLE

rainbow craft

⊞ The flood story is like the rainbow that comes at the end. The story is so serious – and so happy. There are dark clouds of God's judgement and a bright rainbow of God's love.

[Tell the wonderful story of Noah's boat. Remind people that this really happened. It was probably the first ever boat. And it was so big! It was as big as a large ship today. Tell how the animals went into the ark, as God said (Genesis 7:14-16). God saved them all from the terrible flood!]

What a wonderful plan! Only God could do that. All Noah had to do was to **trust** God, and do as God said. Only then did God save him.

⟩⟩ The ark is like Jesus. Jesus is the only way that we can escape God's judgement. We are so bad, but God is so good. He has given us an 'ark'. All we have to do is to climb into the ark. All we have to do is to trust Jesus to save us from judgement. Jesus' death is God's wonderful plan. Are you safe in the ark?

replay

animal clay or felt of biscuits?!

*[Handwritten: Word displays — what do they mean?]*

*[Handwritten: Person profile — Abraham]*

# 4 PROMISE!

⊡ **Background**

God made a new start with Noah, a good man. But God knew that sin was not defeated. People were still evil (Genesis 11:1-9). Hundreds of years went by. We do not know if anyone still worshipped the true God. But God had not forgotten his plan. God planned to sort out the sin problem. God planned to make friends with man again. So he chose a man called Abram (later called Abraham) and gave him a promise.

📖 *Genesis 12:1-9*

This promise is a very serious promise called a **covenant**. God repeats it a few times to Abraham. God adds more details. (📖 *Genesis 17:3-8.* See also Genesis 13:15-17; 15:1-6, 18; 22:15-18.) He also gives the same promise to Abraham's son (Isaac) and grandson (Jacob or Israel).

**The rest of the Bible is about how God keeps this promise. It is God's plan to save the world from sin.**

See how God promises to **bless** This is the opposite of what happened when Adam sinned. Then God **cursed** the world (Genesis 3:17).

• God's **curse** meant **broken** friendship with God, **no home** with God, and **death**.

• God's **blessing** means **new friendship** with God, a **new home** with God and **life for ever**!

⊡ **Main point**

God promises to **bless** his **people** in a **home land**.

✦ **Something to work on**

This promise helps you to understand the whole Bible. Think a lot about it. See how it fits the big story: *Creation – sin – **promise** – Jesus – new creation.*

⊡ **Notes**

**Genesis 12:3**. 'all the nations'. This promise is not just for people who come from Abraham's family line. It is for the whole world. Jesus will come from Abraham. God will bless the world through Jesus (Galatians 3:16).

**Genesis 17:8**. 'land of Canaan'. God promises a home for his people to live in. God meant much more than the little country of Canaan. Abraham's 'descendants' (people from Abraham's family) are people who trust in Jesus. Abraham knew that God has a better 'country' for believers.

📖 *Hebrews 11:8-16*

*[Handwritten: what does it really mean]*

*[Handwritten: Israel / Palestine current situation]*

26

# BLESSING!

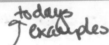

*todays examples*

### 📖 Genesis 12:1-3

Things were bad. People everywhere worshipped false gods. They lived to please themselves. God's world was under God's **curse**. It was spoiled. But then came God's time to **bless**. God chose Abraham. God gave him a promise which was going to change the whole world.

And God's promise to bless Abraham comes all the way down to **us**. God's plan was not only to bless Abraham's family line with the Promised Land. It was specially to bless people **everywhere** with friendship with God (Genesis 12:3).

> ⨂ *God says to us: 'I will bless you through Jesus!' Stop to think how wonderful that is! God's promise to Abraham comes all the way down to us today through Jesus.*

# PEOPLE!

### 📖 Genesis 17:1-7

⊞ Imagine a very old man. God made his promise to Abraham when he was 75 years old. Now Abraham is 99! He still has no son. Will God keep his promise?

It looks impossible! God wants old Abraham to see that only he can give Abraham a son. Only God can bring

nations from Abraham! And he will.

But God also means that another kind of nation will come from Abraham. Abraham will not only have physical children, but spiritual children too. **These are people who believe God's promises, as Abraham did. They are people who believe in Jesus** (who comes from Abraham). The Bible calls Christians 'sons of Abraham' (Galatians 3:7).

# HOME LAND!

### 📖 Genesis 17:8

Canaan never belonged to Abraham. He was always stranger there. It was hundreds of year before his family line (the people of Israel) came to their home. But Abraham was happy with that. He had his eyes on a 'country' that is far better than Canaan.

### 📖 Hebrews 11:9, 10, 16

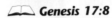

God's promise is not just for the people of Israel and the land of Israel. The story of the Bible is much bigger than that. It tells how God calls people to belong to him. They will become a great 'nation' of people from all round the world. They will know God and live with him for ever, in a home much better than Canaan or even Eden.

> ⨂ *If you want God to bless you like this, you must trust the Person who God promised to Abraham. You must trust Abraham's 'son', **God's** Son, Jesus.*

⑨ – make our own big story cards

Recap day. – Just fun stuff.

This page helps you to understand how God's story fits together. It will help you with the next Bible talk. You can use some of it to help your listeners to understand the Bible story.

Creation

Fall

Promise

Exodus

Creation

### God creates everything good.

God creates the first people. He is friends with them in a beautiful garden. He tells them to have children and to look after his world.

Fall

### Man sins and now cannot be friends with God.

Adam and Eve go against what God told them. The Bible calls this sin. Sin brings death into the world. Now man cannot be friends with God. The perfect world is spoiled. Things get worse and worse. As the years go by, people forget God. After hundreds of years, God judges the world. He kills everything by a flood. He only saves Noah, his family and animals of every kind.

Promise

### God's special promise to Abraham.

After the flood, people sin as before. They forget God again. But this time God does not judge the world. Instead, God has a special plan. God promises to sort out the problem of sin and make people his friends again. He promises them a home land where he will be with them and bless them. The rest of the Bible shows how this happens.

# THE NEXT BIT OF THE STORY

## Genesis 13 - Exodus 1

*[handwritten: Name the sons.]*

**Abraham** had to wait many years for a son. God tested his faith. But God kept His promise. When Abraham was 100 years old, he had a son called Isaac.

**Abraham**

*[handwritten: Peson profiles]*

**Isaac**

**Isaac** had two sons, Jacob and Esau. God called Jacob 'Israel'. God said that he would keep his promise to Abraham through Israel. The people of Israel would become God's special people.

**Jacob** (Israel) had 12 sons. Years later, these became the 12 tribes (families) of Israel.

**Jacob (Israel)**

**12 sons of Israel**

**Joseph**

*[handwritten: Joseph dvd?]*

Jacob's sons did not behave as God's people. The 10 oldest sons hated Joseph. They sold Joseph to be a slave in Egypt. But God was with Joseph. The king ('Pharaoh') made Joseph a ruler of Egypt.

For years, no crops grew. God did this. But Joseph had food because God warned him. He stored grain. Joseph's brothers came to Joseph for food. Then Jacob's whole family came to live in Egypt.

Jacob died. Then Joseph and Jacob's other sons died. By now, there were many children and grandchildren. But a new king forgot Joseph. He made the people of Israel slaves.

*[handwritten: slavery today]*

## Slaves in Egypt

The people of Israel were in Egypt for 400 years. They grew in number until they were about two million. But now they were slaves. Pharaoh was cruel. He did not want the Israelites to become a strong nation. He said that all their baby boys must drown in the river Nile.

But God had not forgotten his promise to Abraham. It was time for God to rescue his people from Egypt. It was time to take them into the special country, the Promised Land. We call this the **Exodus**. (Exodus means 'going out'.)

*[handwritten: explore this word]*

# 5

# RESCUE – SAVIOUR

## ⊡ Background

This background is important for your listeners. Think about the best way to explain it. Pictures may help.

Remember God's special promise to Abraham. This is still God's wonderful plan. But God's people are now in big trouble. For 400 years, they have been in Egypt. They are slaves. And the king is killing all their baby boys.

God chooses **Moses** to save his people from the king of Egypt ('Pharaoh'). So God makes sure that Moses does not die. But also, God plans things so that Moses grows up in Pharaoh's palace!

[In your talk, tell the story of Moses' birth. 📖 **Exodus 2:1-10**. It shows how God is in control.]

40 years later, Moses has to run for his life from Pharaoh. For another 40 years, Moses is a farmer. He looks after sheep in a country called Midian. Then, when Moses is 80 years old, God calls Moses. [Tell the story about the bush 📖 **Exodus 3:1-17**.] God tells Moses: 'You must go back to Egypt to save my people from Pharaoh' (Exodus 3:10).

## ⊡ Main point

God is the strong Saviour. He **will** rescue his people.

## ⊡ Notes

**Exodus 3:3-4.** This bush (small tree) taught Moses some lessons about God. God is like fire. He is holy and burns up sin (Hebrews 12:29). When God spoke, Moses was afraid. But it was also a big honour. God had come down to speak to Moses. God had a special message for him.

**Exodus 3:6, 16.** God's people forget God. But God wants them to know that he is the God of their fathers ('ancestors'). And he is **their** God.

**Exodus 3:8.** This reminds us of God's promise to Abraham. God has not forgotten. God will bring his people to Canaan, the Promised Land.

**Exodus 3:14.** God's special name – I AM. This name is the same as 'Yahweh', 'Jehovah' and 'LORD' (written in capital letters). God's name **shows what he is like.** God wants his people to know how great he is. He is the only God. He always has been God and always will be God. This name is also special for God's people. 'I AM' keeps his promises to them. 'I AM' saves His people.

# GOD RESCUES THROUGH MOSES

 *Exodus 3:10*

**1. God saves people who cannot save themselves.**

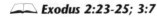 *Exodus 2:23-25; 3:7*

God's people were slaves in Egypt! Pharaoh was cruel. They could not escape. They cried out in their pain. And God heard them. He did not forget his promise. They were still his people. It was time to save them.

> ❯❯ *God saves us when we cannot save ourselves. We need to see that we are slaves to sin. We need to hate our sin. We need to see that we cannot escape. We need to cry to God. Then he will save us.*

**2. God chooses a weak man to save his people.**

 *Exodus 3:11-12*

Moses did not want to go back to Egypt! He could never save the Israelites from Pharaoh! Pharaoh would never let them go! But God said that Moses must go. It was always God's plan. And God promised to be with Moses.

This reminds us of Jesus. God became a man – Jesus – to save us. How can a weak baby born in Bethlehem save us from our sins! How can a weak man on a cross save us! But this is the only way. This is how God chooses to save us.

# GOD HIMSELF RESCUES

 *Exodus 3:8*

God says that **He** has come down to rescue his people. That is so good! He does not only send Moses. **God** comes down to save.

> ❯❯ This is how God saves. It is unlike other religions. We cannot know God by our own efforts. We cannot reach up to God. He **came down** to save us. Jesus came down to die. This is the only way man can be friends with God.

But Pharaoh seems so strong! So God shows **himself** to Moses. Pharaoh is really nothing! ▭ *Exodus 3:14.*

I AM is God's special name. It tells us who he is. He is not like other gods. He is the **only** true God. He is the God who lives. He does what he likes. 'I AM' is also the name that reminds us of God's **promise**. It means that he **will** keep his promise to Abraham. He will save his people.

> ❯❯ *Jesus is also 'I AM'. Jesus is the strong Saviour who is the only God. He has come down to save his people. You must trust Jesus. You are completely safe when you trust this powerful Saviour.*

# 6

# RESCUE – SACRIFICE

## ⊡ Background

God rescues his people from Egypt. This is the big salvation story of the Old Testament. It teaches us how God will save his people through Jesus.

- In Exodus 3, we saw how God comes down to be the **Saviour**.

- In Exodus 12, we see how God saves through **sacrifice**.

Moses obeyed God. He went to Egypt and spoke to Pharaoh: 'God says, "Let my people go"'. Pharaoh did not listen. Instead, he was even more cruel to the Israelites (Exodus 5). God sent many 'plagues' (judgements) to Egypt, but Pharaoh still did not let God's people go (Exodus 7-10).

It is time for the last judgement. God's angel will kill every firstborn (oldest) son. Then Pharaoh will let the Israelites go. (Exodus 11)

But will the Israelite children be safe? Only if they kill a lamb (young sheep). The blood of the lamb will keep them safe.

### 📖 Exodus 12:1-30

This shows how God saved his people. He saved them by a **sacrifice**. A sacrifice is an animal that dies **instead of other people.** This points to Jesus. Jesus is like the lamb (John1:29).

He died instead of sinners, to save us from God's punishment. Now there is no more need for sacrifices. (See next page for more about OLD TESTAMENT SACRIFICES.)

## ⊡ Main point

Trust in God's sacrifice (Jesus). It will keep you safe from God's judgement.

## ⊡ Notes

**Exodus 12:5.** The lamb must not be weak or old (no 'defect' means nothing wrong with it). Only the best lambs were good enough. This reminds us of Jesus:

### 📖 1 Peter 1:19

**Exodus 12:11**. This event and meal is called Passover. This is because the Lord saw the blood and 'passed over' his people's homes (Exodus 12:13). God kept them safe. God told them to eat the Passover meal every year. Jesus is the believer's Passover Lamb. Jesus died at Passover time. The Lord's Supper (Holy Communion) is our Passover meal.

**Exodus 12:12**. 'judgement on all the gods of Egypt.' God showed people in Egypt that their many gods were no good. They couldn't protect anyone against God's punishment. God showed them who the true God is.

📖 **Exodus 12:1-13.** [Tell the story. You could act some of it.]

# GOD JUDGES SIN

📖 **Exodus 12:12**

Pharaoh is fighting against God. God has warned him many times, but he will not listen. At midnight, God goes through Egypt and finds every firstborn son. Each one dies.

📖 **Exodus 12:30**

> ⟫ God is our Judge. We cannot hide from him. God warns us. He is very patient with us. But one day he will come to judge us for our sin. (Romans 2:5-6 explains that when we disobey God, God stores up his anger.)

However, there is one way to be safe:

# GOD PROTECTS SINNERS

📖 **Exodus 12:13**

The Israelites have also sinned. In the past, they have not trusted God. They deserve God to judge them too. But God tells them the way to be safe:

**The blood of the lamb.**

[Describe how the Israelites had to kill a lamb. They put the blood round the door. They stayed inside. God saw the blood and passed over them. The blood of the lamb protected them, because they trusted and obeyed God.]

**The lamb died instead of the son.** The Bible calls this a **sacrifice**.

[Explain more about this. The next page (SACRIFICES) will help you.]

> ⟫ There is a way for us to be safe from God's judgement. **John 1:29.** Jesus came to be our sacrifice. Like the lamb, Jesus was not a sinner. But he died for sinners like us. The way to be safe is to hide under his blood.
>
> Jesus' death was the last sacrifice! There is no other sacrifice to protect you from God's anger. Ask Jesus to be your lamb that died for your sin. Or God's judgement will come on **you**.

# GOD FEEDS HIS PEOPLE

📖 **Exodus 12:8, 11**

God did not only keep his people safe. The Passover lamb that protected them also **fed** them. The food gave them strength for the journey out of Egypt. God saved them to **begin a new life** with him.

> ⟫ Jesus did not only die to save us from God's judgement. He also died to give us new life. Jesus is the Lamb of God and the 'Bread of Life'. As we trust him, he feeds us with everything that we need. He will bring us home to God; **John 6:53-56.**

Sacrifices taught God's people important truths about God. They were like **pictures** for Israel.

People worshipped God with sacrifices right from the beginning. But it was not until God brought Israel out of Egypt that God clearly explained how to worship him. He gave them different sacrifices to teach them truths about God.

You can read what God told them in Leviticus 1-7. (Some study Bibles have helpful charts.)

## Two big picture lessons

When Israel worshipped God, they always had to kill an animal. They burnt the animal on an **altar**. In one way, this did not give God any joy. God does not like seeing death. But the sacrifices were necessary **to teach two big lessons**.

(You can clearly see these lessons in the TALK about the Passover Lamb.)

## 1. Sin deserves death

Sin separates us from God. Remember that is what happened right at the beginning. God told Adam and Eve to go away from him, out of his garden.

There is only one way back to God. Sin must be paid for. And the price of sin is very high. It is **death**.

This is why Israel had to sacrifice animals every day. It was a picture to teach them. Every day they sinned. Every day there had to be **death** to pay for that sin. Only then could they be friends with God.

## 2. Sinners need a sacrifice

The animal did not sin. The people sinned. But the animal died **in the place of the people**.

The sacrifices taught the Israelites that the sacrifice was **in their place**. They needed someone else to die so that they would not have to die.

## Different kinds of sacrifice

All the sacrifices taught the two big picture lessons. But God wanted to teach them **other lessons** too. So each sacrifice also taught another lesson.

This table explains these lessons.

### Example 1: Burnt offering

The priest had to offer a burnt offering every morning and every evening.

They had to burn it **completely**. Not even the priests could eat any.

**Lesson:** *God deserves the whole of our lives. The people should be like a burnt offering, given up completely to him.*

### Example 2: Fellowship (sharing) offering

The **priests** could eat part of many of the other offerings. But the fellowship offering was the only offering that the **people** could share, with God and the priests.

**Lesson:** *The sacrifices show the way to be friends again with God. Once again his people can eat with him. (Think of the Lord's Supper.)*

### Sacrifices and the New Testament

All the sacrifices point to Jesus.

 *Hebrews 10:1-10*

- Animals were only pictures. They could not really take away human sin (Hebrews 10:3-4). Jesus became the real sacrifice. He really did pay the price for sin. (Hebrews 10:8-10)

- The Israelites had to keep making sacrifices, every day. Jesus' death was the one real sacrifice for ever. Jesus made peace with God through his blood (Hebrews 10: 12, 14).

This means that God welcomes everyone who trusts in Jesus! Jesus took the punishment that we deserved. His sacrifice has made us friends with God. We can worship him without fear.

*Hebrews 10:19-24*

# 7 RESCUE – ENEMY JUDGED

## ⊡ Background

God rescues his people out of Egypt. This is the big salvation story of the Old Testament. It teaches us how God will save his people through Jesus.

- In Exodus 3, we saw how God comes down to be the **Saviour**.

- In Exodus 12, we saw how God saves through **sacrifice**.

- In Exodus 14, **God judges the enemy**. God saves his people from their strong enemy.

God always wins against his enemies! But there are three special times in the Bible that God **completely** defeats his enemy. The first one (**the Red Sea**) is an important picture of the other two (the **Cross** and **Judgement Day**).

When God killed all the firstborn sons, Pharaoh told Israel to get out! Then he saw that he had lost all his slaves. So he changed his mind. He chased them with his big army. The Red Sea was in front of the Israelites! The army of Egypt was behind them! They were very frightened.

📖 *Exodus 14*

See MAP (next page).

## ⊡ Main point

We have a strong enemy. God **saves** his people when he **defeats** the enemy.

## ✦ Something to work on

We need to make sure that our talks are more about God than about us.

There are many lessons here. However, the big lesson is about **God**. Israel is in big trouble. Only God can save. Only God's miracle can defeat the enemy. Only **God's** work – Jesus' death and resurrection – can save us from Satan.

## ⊡ Notes

**Exodus 14:4, 17, 18.** Pharaoh has said no to God. His heart is hard. So now God makes his heart even harder. This is so that God will **completely** defeat his enemy. Then everyone will know that he is the true God.

**Exodus 14:21-22.** This was not shallow water. The water made a wall, and later drowned all the Egyptians. It was clearly a miracle.

**Exodus 15.** When God saves, he deserves all the praise.

📖 *Revelation 15:3-4*

## GOD SAVES WHEN IT SEEMS IMPOSSIBLE

📖 *Exodus 14:10*

[Tell the story. The Israelites are very frightened. They cannot escape.]

The Israelites are afraid because they **know how strong the enemy is**.

- What will the Egyptians do to them?

⯈ *We have a strong enemy.* **We** *can do nothing against sin. We are Satan's slaves.* **We** *cannot decide to leave Satan's side and follow Jesus! We must cry out to God to save us! God defeats our strong enemy.*

The Israelites can do nothing. It is time for God to save!

📖 *Exodus 14:13-14*

- What could the Israelites see?

- What did Moses want them to see?

⯈ *God saves when it seems impossible. When you see how bad your sin is,* **look up to God.** *When you are frightened of hell,* **cry out to God.** *Only he can save you.* [Talk about how God defeats sin, Satan and hell – he sent Jesus to die and rise again.]

## GOD DEFEATS THE ENEMY COMPLETELY

📖 *Exodus 14:28-30*

- How many of the Israelites did God save?

- How many of the Egyptians died?

- How did God's people feel afterwards (Exodus 14:31; 15:1-3)?

This story points us to the cross and resurrection of Jesus. **At the Red Sea**, God saved all his people and defeated all his enemies. **On the cross**, Jesus cried out: 'It is finished'. At the cross, Jesus completely **saves**! At the resurrection, Jesus completely **defeats** sin and Satan and hell.

📖 *Hebrews 2:14-15.* [Remind your listeners of the talks on RESCUE.]

⯈ *Has God rescued you yet? Are you like the Israelites on the other side of the Red Sea – safe on God's side? If not, then you are still in great danger. Cry out to Jesus to be your* **Saviour** *and your* **sacrifice**, *and to* **defeat your sin**, *your great enemy.*

- So what did the Israelites do next?

📖 *Exodus 15:1-3*

⯈ *Praise God the Saviour! He deserves all our praise. If we trust in Jesus, we are completely safe. Nothing can separate us from God's love, for ever.*

The Great Sea
(Mediterranean Sea)

Canaan

Egypt

Mount Sinai

40 years wandering in
the desert

Red Sea

0  20  40  60 km

This time line shows dates of some of the main Bible events.

Adam and Eve

Creation

**2000BC**

Abraham

**2000BC** means 2000 years **before Jesus was born**. This is when God gave his special promise to Abraham.

**1400BC**

Land

The Israelites came into the Promised Land after the Exodus. They were there for **1400** years before their Saviour came.

**600BC**
Captivity

About **600BC**, the Israelites were taken away from the Promised Land for about 70 years.

**400BC**
Malachi

The last book of the Old Testament (Malachi) was written about **400BC.** The Bible is silent for 400 years before Jesus comes.

**0**

**0** is when Jesus was born.

Jesus

**60AD**
Good news
goes out

**60AD** means 60 years **after Jesus was born**.
About **60AD**, Paul started to take the good news round the world. Paul and some other apostles began to write the Gospels and the letters.

# 8 10 COMMANDMENTS

## ◉ Background

After 2 months, the Israelites have their first long stop. The people stop by a mountain, called Mount Sinai (See MAP). They are here for nearly a year. God has many things to tell them. He speaks to Moses at the top of the mountain.

The rest of Exodus, Leviticus and Numbers 1-9 tell about the time at Sinai.

The first thing God tells Israel is the **10 commandments** (commands). God makes a **covenant** (special promise) with Israel. He promises to be their God. They must keep his laws. This is the way to live as God's people. (See next page; OLD TESTAMENT LAWS.)

This is a very special time. See how God tells them to get ready:

📖 *Exodus 19*

## ◉ Main point

The 10 commands tell us how God wants his people to live.

## ⊠ Something to work on

📖 *Exodus 20:1-20*

It is easy to make a bad mistake when we teach the 10 commands. We say: 'Try hard to keep these rules and God will be pleased with you'. But we cannot please God this way. Our hearts are full of sin. The way to please God is to believe in Jesus the Saviour.

The 10 commands do two things:

- They show us that we are bad, and we cannot keep God's laws. God wants us to believe in Jesus to rescue us. Jesus is the way to God, not the 10 commands!

- They help God's people to know how to love him and to love one another. 📖 *Matthew 22:36-40*

This sums up the 10 commands.

## ◉ Notes

**Exodus 20:3.** God must be more important than everything else.

**Exodus 20:4.** We must never use images or pictures to worship God.

**Exodus 20:7.** God's name is holy. We must **honour** him when we use his name.

**Exodus 20:8-11.** God created us. He gave us a pattern to follow. He tells us to rest for a whole day each week. It is a holy day, set apart for God.

Many people think like this: 'If I do my best, then God will be happy'. But we must listen to how **God** wants us to live! 10 lessons about the 10 commandments!

## 1. They teach us to love God.
📖 **Exodus 20:1-11.** A Christian is not someone who just keeps the rules. A Christian **knows God**. The first 4 commands teach us how to **love our God**. The 10 commands are all about love.

📖 **Matthew 22:36-40**

## 2. They teach us to love each other.
📖 **Exodus 20:12-17.** We only want to do this when **God** is first in our lives. We will not really love each other unless we love God (Mark 12:29-31).

## 3. They are about our thoughts.
God does not want his people only to be good on the outside! He wants us to please him in our hearts.

📖 **Matthew 5:27-28**

## 4. There are 10.
Which ones do you think are not so important? God says that all 10 of them are important. What we think must change.

## 5. There are not only 10.
God gave his people hundreds of laws! They helped God's people to please God in every part of life. They helped God's people think like this: 'How can I please God best?'

## 6. They make us feel small.
📖 **Exodus 20:18.** They are not a dull list of rules. They are about **God**! What did that mountain teach the people about God's commands?

## 7. They are for us today.
God has not changed! People have not changed! God wants us to live in the same way today. Think about all the problems round us today. How do the 10 commands answer these problems?

## 8. They are for believers.
Remember that God has just saved Israel! 📖 **Exodus 20:2.** The 10 commands teach God's people how to please him. They are not the way to become a Christian!

## 9. They speak to everyone.
Everyone should live in God's way. But that is impossible. Have you obeyed all God's commands? No! So you feel bad. God's commands show us that we cannot please God. We need Jesus!

## 10. They point us to Jesus!
We cannot keep the 10 commands. We cannot be good. The answer is not 'try harder.' The answer is Jesus. Only Jesus can make us friends with God. Jesus always pleased God. Jesus died to take our sin away and give us his goodness. Jesus is the way to know God! Go to Jesus. Jesus will give us a new heart so that we want to please God.

# EXTRA: OLD TESTAMENT LAWS

Some Christians think that the 10 Commands are the only Old Testament laws for us to follow. They think that the other laws were just for Israel. Is this right?

No! Jesus said that he did not come to **do away** with the law. He came to **fulfil it**.

📖 *Matthew 5:17-19*

This means that all the Old Testament laws are **important** for Christians today. It does **not** mean that we must **keep them in the same way**. We must ask why God gave the laws in the first place.

## Two important questions to ask

• What did this law teach the people then?

• So what does it teach Christians now?

---

### EXAMPLE 1: Food laws, Leviticus 11.

The Israelites must not eat some animals (like pigs).

• *What did this law teach the people then?* 📖 *Leviticus 11:45.* They must not be the same as the nations round them. They must be holy for God.

• *What does it teach Christians now?* God still wants his people to be

holy! We must not live like the people round us because we belong to the Lord.

Christians do **not** show this by what they eat. Jesus said that all food is 'clean' now that he has come (Mark 7:19).

So when we read Leviticus 11, we do not worry about what we eat! But we do pray about our lives. Are we holy? Do we say no to sin?

---

### EXAMPLE 2: "an eye for an eye", 📖 *Exodus 21:23-25*

• *What did this law teach the people then?* The man who hurts another person should receive the same hurt. This is not about hate or revenge. It teaches that God is fair. He wants us to be fair. So the law of Israel said "an eye for an eye".

• *So what does it teach Christians now?* God still loves justice. God still wants us to be fair with other people. Jesus also teaches us to **forgive** (Matthew 5:38-39). He does not want us to hit back at people who have hurt us.

Altar of burnt offering

Bowl for washing (laver)

Outer fence

**Tent of Meeting**

**Most Holy Place**
This contained the ark (covenant box) behind a thick curtain.

## The Tabernacle

This tent was where God promised to meet with his people. They offered sacrifices here. They carried the Tabernacle on their journey.

This picture will help you in the next **TALK**. You can make a big picture for your listeners. Show them the ark (covenant box), where God promised to meet the people. But show the thick curtain in front of the Most Holy Place. This separates everyone from God.

## The Temple

Many years later, Solomon built a **Temple**. This was like the Tabernacle, but was a strong and beautiful building, not just a tent.

# 9

# TABERNACLE – GOD WITH US

## ◉ Background

God cannot be with sinful people. We saw this at the Fall, when Adam and Eve went against God. God sent them out of his garden. But God promised Abraham that he **will** be with his new people, Israel.

So there is a big problem: 📖 *Exodus 33:3.* God is holy. The people are full of sin. How can God live with his people?

**The Tabernacle** (special tent – see PICTURE) begins to answer this question. 📖 *Exodus 25:8-22.* We will see that the Tabernacle is not the complete answer. We need **Jesus** before we can come close to God.

The final answer is in **heaven!**

📖 *Revelation 21:3*

## ◉ Main point

The holy God makes a way to live among his sinful people.

## ⊠ Something to work on

Many people think that God does not mind how we worship him. They think that God will be pleased, as long as they are sincere and mean what they say. This is very wrong!

Because we are sinful, the holy God cannot accept us as we are. The only way to worship God is the way he says.

In the Old Testament this was through sacrifices at the Tabernacle. This was a picture of the true way to God, **through Jesus**. This is the only way that takes our sin away, so that God can be with us (Mark 15:37-38).

## ◉ Notes

**Exodus 25:8.** The Tabernacle (tent) was to be a holy house ('sanctuary') for God. It was a tent so that they could move it easily. God would live there among them, in the middle of their tents. (But 📖 *1 Kings 8:27!*)

**Exodus 25:9.** They had to make it **just** as God said. Only God can tell us the right way to worship him.

**Exodus 25:10-22.** The '**ark**' (covenant box) was the most important thing in the Tabernacle. It was a small gold box. In it were the 10 commands, written on two stones. This box had a special lid, with gold angels ('cherubim'). There, above the covenant commands, God promised to speak to his people.

⊕ It is very cold. You must make a fire. But a fire can burn you. You have to be careful. You have to control your fire.

⊗ *Do you want God to be with you? Think carefully! We need God. But God is holy. He is like that fire. He burns up sin. And you cannot control God.*

God's people must have God with them! The Promised Land will be no good without God. But they are afraid of God. God is too holy. They are too sinful.

So God says: 'Build me a house'. It will be a special tent, or **Tabernacle**.

# TABERNACLE – GOD WITH US

📖 *Exodus 25:8*

Of course, God does not fit inside a tent! But God's message is clear. He wants to be with them! He wants them to know that he is with them.

**But there is a big problem.**

⊕ Imagine a child who has a mother who is always at home, but he can never see her! She is always behind a door. A sign says DO NOT COME IN.

It was like that with God. No one could see the ark, where God promised to be (Exodus 25:22). A big, thick curtain was in the way

(Exodus 26:33-34). No one could get near God. [Show this with a picture of the Tabernacle]. Not even Moses could go in where God was!

📖 *Exodus 40:34-35*

⊗ *Do you cry out to **know God**? It is not good enough to go to church, sing the songs. You do not want a God 'behind a curtain'. You must have God close!*

What is the answer? How can sinners be close to our holy God?

# JESUS – GOD WITH US

In the Old Testament God gave part of the answer! He gave Israel **priests** and **sacrifices** so that sinful people could worship their holy God. But God never meant that to be the whole answer. They pointed to **Jesus**.

Jesus is the real Tabernacle. He is God with us. Only Jesus can bring our holy God close to sinful people. Only Jesus kept all God's laws. Only Jesus became the sacrifice to pay for all our sins. On the cross, Jesus tore apart the curtain that keeps us away from the holy God.

📖 *Mark 15:37-38*

⊗ *Do you really want God to live close to you? Do you want to know him, now and for ever? God has come down to us in Jesus. Ask Jesus to bring you close to God.*

# 10

# UNBELIEF

## ◉ Background

At Mount Sinai, God told his people many things. They made the Tabernacle. After a year, the Israelites moved on from there. They travelled towards the Promised Land.

In Numbers 13-14, Moses sent 12 men ('spies') to explore the Promised Land. They found out about the cities, the people, and the land. But they found a big problem…

**Their own unbelief** – they would not believe God. Many times already the Israelites had not trusted God. Will they trust him to take them into the Promised Land?

### 📖 *Numbers 13-14*

## ◉ Main point

We will not receive God's promises if we do not believe and obey God.

## ✦ Something to work on

Fear can be a very big problem. Fear makes things look much worse than they are. Fear can hold us back in our Christian life. Fear can keep some people back from trusting Jesus. Think how this story helps us to face our big fears, with God's help.

Most Christians have fears and doubts. This does not mean that they will not go to heaven! These people did not go into the Promised Land because they **refused** to go forward with God.

## ◉ Notes

**Numbers 13:27**. The land 'flows with milk and honey' (it is 'rich and fertile'). This means that the land is very good. It will produce good crops.

**Numbers 13:33.** The 'Nephilim' ('Anakim') are giants (very, very big people.)

**Numbers 14:9.** Learn from Joshua and Caleb. Because 'the Lord is with us', there is no need to fear. The enemy is strong, but with God, it will be possible to defeat them.

**Numbers 14:9, 11.** See how bad unbelief is. When we will not trust God, we go **against** him ('rebel'). We push God away ('treat God with contempt' or 'reject' God).

**Numbers 14:20-25.** Although God will forgive them, they cannot enter the Promised Land. This is because they **never had** true faith in God.

[Tell the story of the 12 men from Numbers 13. It is a good story to act out. Show the big difference between the 10 frightened men and Caleb and Joshua.]

# WE CANNOT GO IN!

 **Numbers 13:31**

[Numbers 13:27-33. Talk about the strong cities and the giant men. Talk about why the Israelites felt like 'grasshoppers' (small insects).]

- What was their mistake?
- Why did Caleb and Joshua say: 'We can' (Numbers 13:30, 14:6-9)?

> Have you ever thought like this? – 'The Christian life is too hard and I am too weak. I cannot do it!' That is like the 10 men. Our mistake is that we **look at the wrong things**. So we become afraid. [Think of examples.]
>
> Like Caleb and Joshua, we need to look at **God**. There may be giant problems, but God is much stronger! We are weak, but God has promised!

# WE WILL NOT GO IN!

 **Numbers 14:2-4**

How do the people behave? Are you surprised? God has done many great miracles. It was terrible for Israel when they were slaves in Egypt. Then God rescued them from Pharaoh. He killed all their enemies in the sea. But now they say: 'We will not go into God's land. We want to go back to Egypt!'

Today, something else can be surprising. A girl is sad and guilty. She hears the good news about Jesus. Jesus died to set sinners free. He offers to love and forgive us. But the girl says: 'I will not believe. I will go back to my sin'.

>  Be careful. Unbelief is dangerous. It may start with fear. Then it goes against God. It says: 'I will not trust God. I will go my own way'.

# YOU WILL NEVER GO IN!

 **Numbers 14:20-25**

This is what happens when people **will not** believe. **God** says: 'You will never see my Promised Land'. God made the Israelites wander in the desert for 40 years until they all died. Only their children (and Caleb and Joshua) will enter God's Promised Land.

Why? Because of their terrible sin – unbelief. It is a terrible sin when we **will not trust** God.

> Caleb and Joshua were so different! They did not listen to their fears. They trusted God. And they entered the Promised Land. Follow their example.

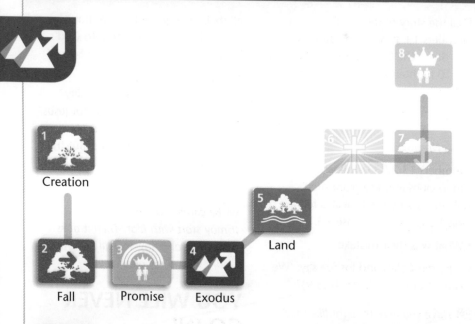

The idea of **LAND** is there from the beginning –
God is friends with Adam and Eve in a beautiful garden
**(LAND)**.

Creation

Adam and Eve go against what God told them. Now man
cannot be friends with God. God throws them out of the garden
**(LAND)**.

Fall

God promises Abraham that he will make people friends with
him again. He promises them a home **LAND**, to be with them
and bless them.

Promise

God's people are slaves in a foreign land. God rescues them to
bring them to the Promised **LAND**.

Exodus

God brings his people into the Promised **LAND**. Here God
promises to be with his people and bless them, if they follow him.
But will this happen? There is still the problem of their sin...

Land

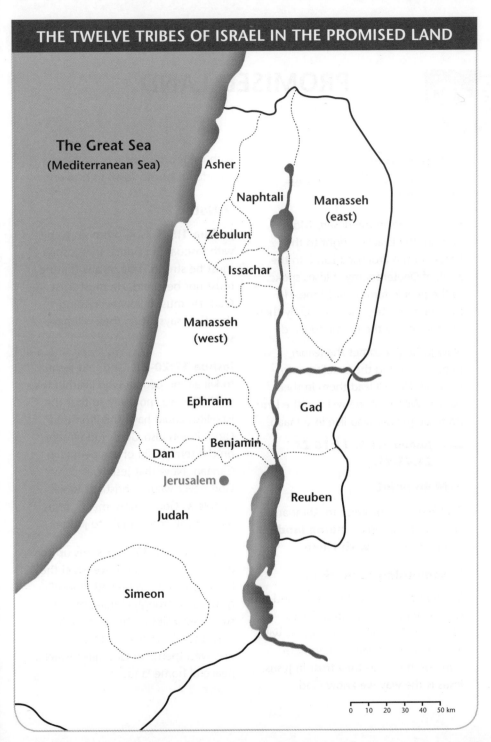

# THE TWELVE TRIBES OF ISRAEL IN THE PROMISED LAND

**The Great Sea**
(Mediterranean Sea)

Asher

Naphtali

Manasseh
(east)

Zebulun

Issachar

Manasseh
(west)

Ephraim

Gad

Benjamin

Dan

Jerusalem ●

Reuben

Judah

Simeon

0 10 20 30 40 50 km

# 11

# PROMISED LAND

## ◉ Background

(See STORY SO FAR on the page before this.)

After 40 years in the desert, Moses brought the Israelites right to the border of the Promised Land. In the book of Deuteronomy, Moses spoke to the people for one last time. He told them to obey the Lord. Only then can they enjoy the Promised Land.

Now Joshua becomes the leader. Joshua will bring the Israelites into the land. He will lead them in their battles. With God, he will win the land from the people who live in Canaan.

📖 *Joshua 1:1-9; 11:16-23; 21:43-45.*

## ◉ Main point

God keeps his promise to Abraham. He gives his people a **home land** where he will be **with them**.

## ⊡ Something to work on

Remember that the Promised Land is only **part** of God's promise to Abraham. The full answer comes with Jesus. Believers today enjoy these same promises, as they trust in Jesus. Jesus is the way we know God with us. Jesus is the way we have a wonderful **home land** in heaven.

## ◉ Notes

**Joshua 1:5-9.** God promises to be with Joshua. But notice that Joshua must be strong. This means that he must not be afraid. He must trust God. He must follow everything that God says. Then they will have success.

**Joshua 11:20-21.** God told Joshua to kill all the people who lived in the land. This was not only so that the Israelites could have the Promised Land. It was also God's judgement on the terrible sin of the people in Canaan. Now that Jesus has come, God never wants Christians to kill people as God's 'judgement'. Jesus himself will come again to judge.

**Joshua 21:43-45.** This sums up the book of Joshua. God gave Israel the Promised Land, as he had 'sworn' (promised strongly). None of the strong enemies in the land could defeat the Israelites because God was with them. So God gave Israel a peaceful home land.

# GOD IS WITH THEM

📖 *Joshua 1:9*

At last! After all those years in the desert, the Israelites are going to have their own home land! God's people will live in their own houses and work their own land. They will enjoy this good land that God gives them.

But God promises them something much better than good things! **God himself will be with them.**

---

⟫ *Which one do you want most? Which is the **best** thing?*

- *For God to give you many good things?*
- *For God himself to be with you?*

*God may give us many **difficult** things, but if God is with us, we can face them all.*

---

There is another important reason why God will be with them. **He will fight their enemies with them.** The people in the land are strong. They fight well. The Israelites cannot win on their own. But with God on their side, they cannot lose!

---

⟫ *This is a great promise for believers. The Christian life is too hard for us. Sin and Satan are too strong for us to fight on our own.*

---

*But look at God's promises in*
📖 *Hebrews 13:5-6*
📖 *Ephesians 6:10-11*

# GOD GIVES THEM A HOME LAND

📖 *Joshua 21:43-45*

Imagine it! The Israelites had to fight for every town. They had to fight every tribe. War! War! War!

It can often feel like that when we follow Jesus. It is so hard. Will it ever get easy? Yes! God did not give the Israelites the Promised Land so that they had to fight all the time. He gave them a **home land**. It was to be a land of rest and peace and joy. God gave them each their own piece of good land to live on. It was their home, with God.

God kept his promises to Abraham. He gave his people a home land where he will be with them.

---

⟫ *God keeps his promises to us today. Life may seem hard, but God promises you **rest** in your heart when you trust Jesus.*
📖 *Matthew 11:28-30*

*Life as a Christian may seem hard, but God promises **rest** for his people, with him for ever! [Talk about what being at home with God for ever will be like.] Can you say what Paul says in* 📖 *Romans 8:18?*

# 12

# FALSE GODS

## ◉ Background

See next page for more, important background.

God gave his people everything that they needed; good land and God's presence. But the Israelites had two big sins which meant that they did not enjoy God's Promised Land. These are deep sins of the human heart. They are in us too.

- **Unbelief** (we saw that in Numbers 13-14)

- **False gods**

📖 *Judges 2*

**Judges 2** sums up the book of the Judges. It shows that Israel will not give up their false gods (idols). It shows God's anger – but also his help. God punishes Israel by the enemies round them. Then God, in love, sends leaders ('judges') to rescue his people from their enemies. But the Israelites do not learn. They still love their false gods.

## ◉ Main point

God's people show their love for false gods. God is angry – and loving.

## ⊠ SOMETHING TO WORK ON

It seems so stupid to worship false gods. They are nothing and God is everything (Jeremiah 2:11, 13). **So why do God's people love idols?**

Work hard at this question. Then it will help God's people today to see the things that are 'false gods' in their own lives.

## ◉ Notes

**Judges 2:2-3.** God told the Israelites to kill **all** their enemies. But they did not obey. They allowed some of their enemies to stay in the land. This was the big problem. Their enemies worshipped idols. Then the Israelites started to worship the idols too.

**Judges 2:10-13.** As time went by, the Israelites started to love the false gods – like Baal and Ashtoreth. People thought that they had power to give **life**! They prayed to them for good crops and success.

**Judges 2:16.** These 'judges' did not sit in courts. They were **rulers** or **leaders** for Israel. They put their faith in God. They fought the enemy and rescued Israel. They point to Jesus, who came to save us from our enemies.

# GOD'S PEOPLE LOVE FALSE GODS!

⊕ You are thirsty. What would you choose to drink? Fresh, clean water from a well? Or warm, muddy water with germs in it?

When we choose false gods, we choose the 'muddy water.' That is so **wrong** and so **foolish**.

📖 *Jeremiah 2:11, 13*

• Why do we do this?

## 1. We want to get on

📖 *Judges 2:2-3*

Israel did not want to fight the rest of their enemies. They wanted to be at peace with them. Israel started to copy how they lived in this land. So Israel began to worship their gods – it seemed the best way to get on in life.

> ➢ *We want people to like us. We want to have money. We do not want to be different from the people round us. So we copy them. We like the things that they have. We want their idols. But this is not God's way. The way to get on **as a Christian** is to trust and obey God.*

## 2. Sin is so strong
📖 *Judges 2:19*

They just would **not** give up their sin! Sin is so strong. It is deep in our hearts. It tempts us to go away from God. We need Jesus' power to set us free.

# GOD IS ANGRY – AND LOVING

What will God do? He has saved his people. He has given them the Promised Land. But they have turned away from him!

## God is angry

📖 *Judges 2:14, 15*

God punishes them! He fights against them! This is because he cares for them so much.

> ➢ *Praise God that he does not leave his people to go away from him! God may hurt us – but that is because he loves us.* 📖 ***Hebrews 12:5-6.*** *Have you gone away from God? Have you loved false gods? Will you say sorry and come back to God today?*

## God is loving
📖 *Judges 2:16*

God brings trouble on Israel. Then he gets them out of trouble! He sends them leaders to fight the enemy and set them free.

> ➢ *God loves to save us from our sin! This is why he sent Jesus his Son. The judges could never really rescue Israel, but Jesus truly does bring sinners back to God!*

With God, Joshua defeated the enemies in the Promised Land and gave the Israelites peace. But there were still enemies in the land. God gave the 12 tribes of Israel their own area of the land. Then he told them to kill the enemies.

But Israel found it hard to kill all the enemies. They did not ask God for help. They stopped trying (Judges 1:27-36).

The picture shows what happened next.

**1** Israel worships false gods (Judges 2:12)

**2** God hands Israel over to their enemies (Judges 2:14)

**3** Israel are in big trouble (Judges 2:15)

**4** God saves them by a leader (Judges 2:16)

**5** Soon, Israel goes back to their idols (Judges 2:17)

**6** Israel gets worse and worse (Judges 2:19)

**Again and again**

Things went wrong so quickly. God's people spoiled God's good land. This is because they loved their idols and wanted their own way.

The book of Judges shows that God loves to save his people. But none of the judges can save Israel for very long. They point us to Jesus. Jesus will change people's hearts. He will set them free from their sin.

*Judges 21:25.* What is the next part of God's plan for his people? He will give them a **king**...

The next three important people are Samuel, Saul and David.

### Samuel – Prophet

 *1 Samuel 3:19–21*

God's message to Israel came through Samuel.

- Samuel showed Israel their sin.
- Samuel taught Israel God's truth.

### Saul – King

The people's choice

 *1 Samuel 8:19-21*

- Samuel led the people well, but the people wanted to have a king. They wanted to be like the nations round them. That means that they did not want God to rule over them.
- Saul was tall and strong. He could have made a good king. But he did not obey God. So God said that Saul could not be king any more.

### David – King

God's choice

*1 Samuel 16:13*

Out of love, God gave his people a good king.

- God chose David to lead Israel in God's ways. He brought them God's rule.
- David is a picture of Jesus the King. We need Jesus as our King. Jesus brings God's rule over our lives.

# 13

# GOD'S KING!

## ⊡ Background

See STORY FILL-IN on the page before this.

David is king. He has defeated the enemies round God's people. They now live in peace. David is a good and just king. He leads the people in God's ways.

### 📖 2 Samuel 8:14-15

The centre of Israel's worship is still just a tent – the Tabernacle that they made in the desert. In 2 Samuel 7, David wants to build God a great Temple. He wants to honour God.

God is pleased with David, but he has better plans. David's son, Solomon, will build the Temple. But God has wonderful plans for King David.

Now we learn about these wonderful plans for his king. We see how God keeps his promise to Abraham. King David is another step towards the rule of King Jesus.

### 📖 2 Samuel 7:1-17

## ⊡ Main point

When God's King is over us, we enjoy God's wonderful promises.

## ⊡ Something to work on

What does it mean to have God's King over us? It is easy to say that Jesus is our King, but does he rule our lives? Help your listeners to think about this. For example, if Jesus is our King, do we do **everything** that he asks? Do we really believe that he knows best? Do we put our will under his?

## ⊡ Notes

**2 Samuel 7:11-16.** David wants to build God a 'house', but God promises to give **David** another kind of 'house', a **kingdom**! (Other words for this – 'throne', 'dynasty'.) God's plans for King David are so much bigger than David's plans for a Temple!

**2 Samuel 7:12.** David will of course die, but this will not end David's kingdom. Although future kings will fail (2 Samuel 7:14), God promises David a kingdom that will never end (2 Samuel 7:16).

# WHEN GOD'S KING RULES

⊕ [Talk about what happens when different leaders are in charge of your country. What is it like when leaders are greedy and selfish? What is it like when they are fair and want the best for their people?]

📖 **2 Samuel 8:14-15.** King David changes the whole country! Now they have peace, not war. Things are fair. Why is this?

**Because David follows God's laws.** David does not do what he thinks is best. He does what **God has written**. He leads the people in the way God says is right.

> ⊠ *The only good Ruler for your life is God. Think carefully. Is he your boss? Does his word rule you – or do you do what **you** think is best?*

# PROMISES!

📖 **2 Samuel 7:8-16**

God makes David some wonderful promises. These promises point us to Jesus. The Old Testament says that another 'King David' will come. That means Jesus.

## 1. A home for ever

📖 **2 Samuel 7:10**

We have had this promise before! But the Israelites' sin spoiled the home that God gave them. God promises that David's kingdom will bring God's people a home for ever. Nothing will spoil it.

## 2. God with them for ever

📖 **2 Samuel 7:13**

David's son, Solomon, will build a Temple. This means God wants to **stay** with his people. In the new heaven and new earth they will worship God for ever (Revelation 21:3).

## 3. A throne for ever

📖 **2 Samuel 7:16**

Israel had judges for a time. But kings were here to stay. God's plan for his people is **always** to have a king, like David, to rule over them.

After a time, it looked as if everything had gone wrong again. Most of Israel's kings did not rule well like David. Israel was in trouble again. But God's promises did not fail. They pointed forward to King Jesus. Jesus gives his people these three blessings, that God promised to David.

> ⊠ *Think carefully about the three wonderful promises. Do they belong to you because you have Jesus as your King? If you are not sure, will you bow to King Jesus today? Will you ask him to forgive you and rule over your life?*
> 📖 *Isaiah 55:3*

The next king after David was his son, Solomon.

## Solomon

• He built the Temple (1 Kings 6).

• God made him the wisest man ever (1 Kings 10:23).

• God made his kingdom very rich and peaceful (1 Kings 4:25).

• **But Solomon went after false gods!** (1 Kings 11:1-13)

So Solomon spoiled God's kingdom. God was angry. He split Israel into two kingdoms. These were now called:

• **Israel** (10 tribes in the north)

• **Judah** (2 tribes in the south)

Judah was the tribe of David. God kept his promises to David through this tribe. Jesus was born into the tribe of Judah.

From then on, God's people were in two groups. Israel and Judah had different kings.

They often fought each other.

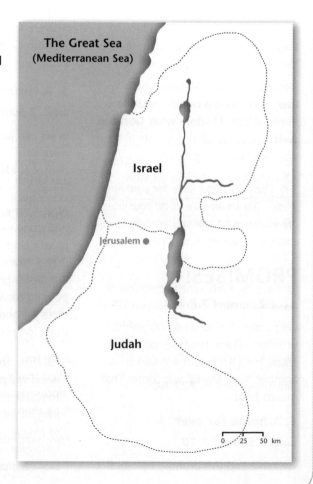

The Great Sea
(Mediterranean Sea)

Israel

Jerusalem

Judah

0    25    50 km

## Israel's bad kings

**Jeroboam** was the first king.

He made golden calves (idols) for Israel to worship.

**Israel's kings got worse and worse**

None of them followed God. **King Ahab** was one of the bad kings of Israel.

Over about 200 years, 20 bad kings ruled over Israel. God's people went further and further away from God.

In the end, God sent the nation of **Assyria** against Israel. Assyria killed many of the people. They captured many other people and took them away to Assyria.

This happened in **722 BC.**

## Judah's bad and good kings

**Rehoboam** was the first king.

He led Judah away from God.

**Judah's kings: some were good, some were bad**

Some kings, like **Jehoshaphat**, **Hezekiah** and **Josiah**, tried to lead Judah back to God. Other kings, like **Ahaz** and **Manasseh**, led Judah to worship idols.

Over about 350 years, 20 kings ruled over Judah. Although some of them were good, God's people still went further and further away from God.

In the end, God sent the nation of **Babylon** against Judah. Babylon killed many of the people. They captured many other people and took them away to Babylon.

This happened in **586 BC.**

# 14

# A SONG OF TRUST

This talk takes a break from the history of the Old Testament. This is because God speaks in other ways too. God speaks through the songs and wise words of the Bible. Psalm 91 is an example.

## ▣ Background

David wrote many of the psalms. He may have written Psalm 91. It helps God's people whenever they are afraid. 📖 *Psalm 91.*

## ◉ Main point

If you trust in God, there is no need to fear.

## ✴ Things to work on

**1.** This psalm does not mean that bad things will never happen to God's people. It does mean that God's people do not need to be **afraid** of bad things. This is because God promises to look after us. He says: 'I will be with [them] **in trouble**' (Psalm 91:15). God makes the bad things work for our good. Psalm 91 is like 📖 *Romans 8:28-39.*

**2.** The psalm does **not** mean that Christians can do dangerous things and be safe. It is not safe to fight lions and snakes (Psalm 91:13). We

must not **test** God's care for us. We must **trust** God's care for us 📖 (Luke 4:9-12).

## ◉ Notes

**Psalm 91:2, 4.** 'refuge', 'fortress', 'shield', 'rampart' (defence). These are all pictures of God's **protection** against enemies. God is a safe place like a castle (refuge, fortress). We can hide in him and be safe. A shield protects against arrows.

**Psalm 91:3.** 'fowler's snare' - a trap to catch birds. 'pestilence' - disease.

**Psalm 91:7-8.** God's people are safe when they trust in God's protection. But God does not keep wicked people safe from these dangers. He punishes them.

**Psalm 91:13.** Remember that this is **poetry**. Poetry uses pictures to mean other things. This verse reminds us of the devil and evil spirits. Jesus has trodden on Satan's head (Genesis 3:15). So Jesus' people are safe from evil spirits when they trust in him.

**Psalm 91:16.** Some Christians die young. This is not because they do not trust God. But after death God gives his people life for **ever**!

# NO NEED TO FEAR

What things are you afraid of? [Talk about this in groups.] Why are you afraid of these things?

- 📖 *Psalm 91:3-6, 13.* Talk about these dangers. What other dangers do they remind you of? Are you afraid of these things?

⊕ Often we are afraid of things that we **cannot see**. When you go out in the dark, perhaps something will attack you. You cannot see.

Many of the dangers in the psalm are hidden things. We are afraid because we do not know if these things will suddenly hurt us.

> ⟫ *This psalm says: 'There is no need to fear!' What a great joy! When we trust God, he promises to look after us. God is in control of all the things that we are afraid of. Think again of the things that you are afraid of. God says: 'I will keep you safe from all of them'. Will you trust him?*

# TRUST IN GOD!

Psalm 91 is a great comfort because it tells us **why** we can trust God!

### Pictures

Talk about these beautiful pictures of God. Why do they make us feel so safe?

- 📖 *Psalm 91:1, 2, 4.* God is a safe place like a castle. We can hide in him and be safe. Attacks and arrows cannot hurt us.

- 📖 *Psalm 91:4.* God is like a strong mother bird. We are weak, like baby birds. But God's wings cover us from danger when we trust in him.

### Promises

- 📖 *Psalm 91:9-16.* How many promises can you count in this section? Again and again, God says: 'I **will** look after you'. He tells his angels to watch over his people (Psalm 91:11). Dangers and trouble may come, but they cannot touch us unless God says so. God is in control.

> ⟫ *So trust in God! See how God promises his protection **when we trust in him** (Psalm 91:9, 14, 15). We are safe when we love him and pray to him.*
>
> *Now will you let go of the fears you thought of, and hide in God?*

**Poetry**. These five books come after the **History** books and before the **Prophets**. They do not tell us the story of what happened. So how do they fit into what God wants us to know?

**They help God's people to live in a way that pleases him. They help us to know God.**

- People sometimes call them 'wisdom' books. They give us much wisdom to live in a way that pleases God.

- They do not tell us straight facts. They are **poetry**. Poetry helps us to say how we **feel**. These books speak in a direct way to us.

- Each book is very different. Each book helps us with different things about how to follow God's ways.

## How to understand these books

### 1. Job: suffering

Job tells a story about a man who suffers. You need to read the whole story to understand Job. For most of the book, Job argues with people who want to help him. This can be hard to follow, but there are many lessons to learn.

**3 lessons from Job**

- God is **in control** of **everything**.

- God has **many** reasons for suffering. Every one is **good**.

- We do not need to understand everything. We do **need** to **trust** God in everything.

**2. Psalms:** song book

There are 150 psalms. David wrote many of them.

- Read a psalm through a few times to understand the main message.

- Think about how the writer is **feeling**. Do you feel like him sometimes?

- Remember that King David points us to King Jesus. Often the psalms will lead us to Jesus.

### Different kinds of psalms (with examples)

- Praise psalms (103)

- Trust psalms (91)

- Trouble psalms (42)

- History psalms (105)

- Sorry psalms (51)

**3. Proverbs:** wise words

The first nine chapters **call** us to listen. We must follow wisdom's ways. We must not listen to another dangerous voice which calls us away from God.

- For the rest of the book, wise words are mostly in verses on their own. You will notice many proverbs on some topics – like money or work.

- Proverbs often talk about two kinds of people – wise and foolish. Which will we be?

'The fear of the Lord is the beginning of knowledge.'

**4. Ecclesiastes:** life's meaning

This is a hard book to understand. Read it all through and think about the whole book. The book has one main message. **Without God, life has no meaning.**

- Notice how the writer repeats verses to make his point.

'It is all useless. It is like chasing the wind.'

**5. Song of Songs:** love songs

Love songs tell the story of Solomon and his bride.

- There are beautiful sections which show how good love is. They remind us of the love that Jesus has for his people.

'My lover is mine, and I am his'.

# 15 THE PROPHETS – JUDGEMENT AND HOPE

## ▣ Background
See next page for more about PROPHETS.

King David ruled Israel in God's ways. 200 years later, God's kingdom has split into **Judah** and **Israel**. God's people are far from God. Many of the kings do not listen to God. (See page 58 – KINGS OF ISRAEL AND JUDAH.)

So God sends the prophets to speak to his people. By now, **Israel** is in big trouble. Assyria has come to punish **Israel**. Assyria has also attacked the towns of **Judah** (Isaiah 1:7). But it is still not too late for **Judah**. The main city, Jerusalem, is still there (Isaiah 1:8). Isaiah speaks to **Judah**. **Judah** must repent and trust God.

## 📖 Isaiah 1, 2:1-4

## ⊙ Main point
God will judge his people for their sin. But God's future plans still give hope.

## ⊛ Something to work on
The message of the prophets is very important for today. Keep to the main points. Show how our sin is like the sin of the people then. Point to Jesus, who gives us hope for the future.

## ▣ Notes
**Isaiah 1:2-4.** Animals know who looks after them. But God's people are evil. They **have turned their backs on** ('rebelled', 'forsaken', 'spurned') their own Master.

**Isaiah 1:11-15.** Judah still keeps up their religion! But God hates their sacrifices and their meetings. This is because he sees their evil hearts.

**Isaiah 1:21-23.** Jerusalem was once a good, fair city. But the people are no longer faithful to God. God calls the city a 'harlot' ('whore') – they are like a woman who is not faithful to her husband. The rulers are unjust. They love money. They do not care for people in need.

**Isaiah 1:24-26.** God calls his own people his **enemies**! He will judge their sin. But this is because he has **good** plans for Jerusalem (Isaiah 1:26).

**Isaiah 2:1-4.** Isaiah uses the picture of Jerusalem, but he speaks of much more than this city! It sounds like God's promises to Abraham. God promises a home land of peace and blessing. People from all nations will come to find a home land here. This points to the blessings that Jesus brings, and to heaven.

# GOD JUDGES SIN

⊞ If you love your children, are you sad when they do wrong? Do you punish them? When you punish them, what do you hope will happen?

God will not let his people go! They are so evil, but he will not give up with them. His love never changes! God is right to be very angry. See how much he hates these sins. [Talk more about each one. Show how these sins can be true of us.]

- God's people have **turned their backs** on their Master.
  📖 *Isaiah 1:2-4*

- God hates their **religion**. It is not real. It disgusts God.
  📖 *Isaiah 1:13-15*

- God hates their **lives**. They do not care about anyone else.
  📖 *Isaiah 1:23*

So God is against them. He warns that he will send enemies to attack them. But why does God say all this? What does he want them to do?

**God wants them to repent!**
📖 *Isaiah 1:16-20*

God wants to forgive them! He wants them to come back to him. He longs to take their dirty sin and wash it all away. He wants to bless them again in their land. He does not want to send the enemy to punish them!

▷▷ *Have you turned your back on your Master? Does he hate the way you pretend to worship? Does he hate the way you live? Then listen to God's warning! And turn back to him. He loves to wash us clean again.*

# GOD GIVES HOPE

📖 *Isaiah 2:1-4*

Sadly, God's people did not listen. God had to send Babylon against Judah. **But God still will not give up on his people.**

The book of Isaiah is full of promises about God's future for his people. After God has judged them, he will send a Saviour. He will give them a home land. He will bless them, as he promised Abraham.

📖 *Isaiah 2:1-4*

⊞ Think of the best place in the world to live. Everything is perfect! This is far better! What a beautiful picture! What a happy place! How safe and peaceful it is! See how all the people from all over the world want to come there! They want to come to worship God.

▷▷ *If you know Jesus, heaven is your home land. There will be no more tears and trouble. There will only be joy and love, with Jesus for ever. Life may be hard now, but remember heaven!* 📖 *Revelation 21:22-27*

The books of the prophets take up a large part of the Bible (from Isaiah to Malachi). The prophets can be hard to understand, but they are very important!

## Why God sent the prophets

God sent prophets when the kings did not listen to God's word.

The kings had God's laws to follow. But often they took no notice of God's laws. So God sent the prophets. The prophets are like policemen. They say: 'You do not keep God's law. If you will not change, then God will punish you.'

## God sent the prophets to tell about the future.

- God's prophets tell how God will punish God's people and other nations.

- God's prophets tell about God's future plans to bless God's people.

The future promises can be hard to understand. They often speak about three things **at the same time**:

1. God's promise to bring the people of Israel back home to Jerusalem.

2. God's promise to send a Saviour, to rescue people from sin.

3. God's promise to bring his people home to heaven.

Promises about Jerusalem are often pictures of the other two promises.

## Who the prophets spoke to

- **Hosea**, **Amos** and **Jonah** spoke to **Israel**. (Other famous prophets to Israel were Elijah and Elisha. They did not write books.)

- Most of the other prophets spoke to **Judah**.

## When the prophets spoke

The prophets wrote their books over about 300 years. It is important to understand the time in history. Only then can we understand their message. (A study Bible will help you.)

- Many prophets spoke **before** God sent Assyria and Babylon against his people. They warned God's people to repent. But they would not listen.

- Daniel and Ezekiel spoke **in Babylon**. This was when Babylon had taken the people of Judah away from Jerusalem.

- Haggai, Zechariah and Malachi spoke to God's people when they were **back home** again in Jerusalem.

**The timeline on the right shows when some of the main prophets of the Bible spoke and wrote.**

## What the prophets said all happened

- Assyria came to fight **Israel**. They took God's people away to Assyria in 722BC.

- 150 years later, Babylon was the strong power. Babylon came against **Judah** and burnt Jerusalem and the temple in 586BC. They took God's people away to Babylon.

- After 50 years, Persia defeated Babylon. King Cyrus told God's people that they could go back to Jerusalem. They built the temple again. But they did not follow God's ways for long.

- Then there were 400 difficult years for God's people. The Bible says very little about this time. A few believers waited for God to send the promised Saviour.

- Then Jesus came!

**Israel**          **Judah**

**722BC**
Israel taken to Assyria

**Isaiah**
Isaiah tells Judah to repent and trust God. If not, God will send enemies to Judah, as He did to Israel. But there is hope for the future.

**Jeremiah**
Jeremiah tells Judah that God will send Babylon against them.

**586BC**
Judah taken to Babylon

**Daniel and Ezekiel**
These prophets speak to the people of Judah in Babylon.

# 16

# RETURN!

## ⬡ Background

- God punished his people for their sin. Babylon attacked Jerusalem and took the people away (586BC).

📖 *2 Chronicles 36:15-21*

- Years later, Persia defeated Babylon. In 536 BC, God told King Cyrus to let his people go back home.

📖 *2 Chronicles 36:22-23*

- Some Jews went back to Jerusalem. They built the city and the temple. But again, enemies attacked Jerusalem (Nehemiah 1:3).

Nehemiah 1 happens 90 years after the first Jews returned (445BC). It shows how God loves his people to come back home.

Nehemiah prays that the king will let him go back to Jerusalem. He wants to make God's city strong again.

📖 *Nehemiah 1:1-11, 2:5*

## ⬡ Main point

God loves his people to come back to him.

## ✶ Something to work on

This is the last talk from the Old Testament. Show how God has still not fully kept his promises to Abraham. At the end of the Old Testament, God's people are weak. They are under a foreign king. They do not follow God well. They know little of the blessings that God promised them. They need to wait for the Saviour. He will make the promises come true at last!

## ⬡ Notes

**Nehemiah 1:3-4.** Nehemiah has never lived in Jerusalem. He is sad, because Jerusalem is **God's** city. When Jerusalem is broken down, God's people are in trouble. And God is not honoured.

**Nehemiah 1:6-7.** Nehemiah thinks of Israel's past sins as his own sins. He does not say: 'I did not sin!'

**Nehemiah 1:8-10.** Nehemiah reasons from the Bible:

- God promised punishment. But he also promised to bring his people back.

- These are God's own people. He rescued them in the past. Surely he will save them again!

# GOD'S LOVE

⊞ How do you imagine God's **hands**? Are they angry, ready to hit you? Or are they loving? Does God hold them out to say: 'Come'?

### 📖 Isaiah 54:7-8

Yes, God is angry when his people sin. But see how his love is even stronger. God loves his people to come back to him.

Nehemiah prays to this God of love.

### 📖 Nehemiah 1:6, 8-10

- What things does he remember about God? [See notes.]

- How does this encourage us? Why would God want us back when we have sinned?

> ⊠ *You may feel far from God. But look! See God's loving hands and smile. They say: 'Come back! I will forgive you. You are welcome home'* (Luke 15:11-24).

# OUR RETURN

### 📖 Nehemiah 1:6-7

When we come back to God, we are glad because of God's love. But we are sad too.

Nehemiah was very sad at what happened. He looked back. He saw how his people had gone away from God. He saw all those terrible years away in foreign lands. He saw that God's people were **still** weak and in trouble.

> ⊠ *Are you sad? Are you sad at the bad mistakes you made? Are you sad because you made God sad? Are you sad at your **sin**?* 📖 *Nehemiah 1:7*

Nehemiah was not only sad. He **did something**. He wanted to go back home! This is what God's people do. They say sorry and come back home to God! Will you do that now (Hosea 6:1-3)?

# JESUS

Remember God's promises to Abraham. A home land. God will be with them and bless them. People from other nations will come too.

Here, at the end of the Old Testament story, this has still not happened! God blessed his people, but their sin spoiled everything. **They need someone who can change their hearts.** They need someone to save them from their **sin**. They need Jesus. He will make all God's promises come true.

> ⊠ *Jesus is with us today! Do you feel your need of him? He is the only one who can change **your** heart. He calls us: 'Come to me!' Will you come?*

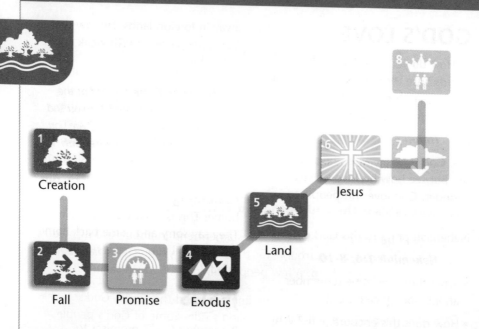

### God creates everything good.

God creates the first people. He is friends with them in a beautiful garden.

Creation

### Man sins and now cannot be friends with God.

Adam and Eve go against what God told them. The Bible calls this sin. Sin brings death into the world. Man can no longer be friends with God. God sends him away.

Fall

### God's special promise to Abraham.

God promises Abraham that he will make people friends with God again. God promises them a home land, where he will be with them and bless them.

Promise

**God rescues his people from Egypt.** The people of Israel are from Abraham's family line. God says that they are his special people. They become slaves in Egypt. God rescues his people from Egypt. They travel to the Promised Land.

Exodus

Land

### God blesses his people in the Promised Land.

God brings his people into the Promised Land. They defeat the Canaanites. God blesses them. But they worship false gods. God gives them trouble from the nations round them. In the end, enemies take God's people away to foreign lands. Later, they return to the Promised Land, but they still sin. They need a Saviour to save them from their sin. They need God's King to rule over their lives.

### This is the end of the Old Testament.

The last books of the Old Testament end in about 400 BC. God's people were in trouble for the next 400 years. Other nations ruled over them. A few people still loved God (Malachi 3:16).

When Jesus was born, the Romans ruled the world. God's people were still not under God's rule. Some of God's people (like Simeon and Anna, Luke 2:25-38) waited for a Saviour and a King. Only he could save them from their sins. Only he could make all the promises of the Old Testament come true.

Then, at last...

Jesus

### God sent Jesus to save people everywhere.

Jesus came to die on a cross and rise from the dead. This is the only answer for our sin. Now God and man can be friends again.

See how Jesus comes near the **end** of the story, not the beginning! When we start with Jesus, we start at the last part of the story. That is not usually a good plan.

**This is why we need to teach the Old Testament.** The Old Testament shows us why we need Jesus. The Old Testament teaches us about how evil the human heart is. It makes us look for the Person who can really save us.

# 17 PROMISED SAVIOUR

### ◉ Background

At last the promised Saviour comes – 2,000 years after God made his promise to Abraham. Through Jesus, all the nations will be blessed. The Old Testament years prepared the way for Jesus. We will look at Luke's story of the good news of Jesus' life, death and resurrection. This will show us how Jesus came as the Old Testament promised.

📖 **Luke 4:14-30.** Jesus begins teaching. He tells the people who he truly is.

### ◉ Main point

Jesus, God's Saviour, has come, as the Old Testament promised.

### ◉ Notes

**Luke 4:16-17.** Jesus comes back to his home town. The people are excited because they have heard good stories about Jesus. When they meet to hear God's word in their synagogue, they ask Jesus to teach them. He takes a 'scroll' (rolled up paper) and reads from Isaiah 61:1-2.

**Luke 4:18-19.** Isaiah 61 speaks about someone who has the Spirit of God. God has 'anointed' (chosen) him. He comes with good news for people in trouble.

- 'The poor': This does not mean people who have no money. It means people who are humble. They know that they need God.

- 'Prisoners' ('captives'): Old Testament Israel was never truly free, because their sin brought them trouble again and again. This Saviour will truly make people free.

- 'Blind': People who do not see their need of God.

- 'The oppressed' are people who suffer under a cruel king. These are people who are in trouble from sin and Satan. They need a Saviour to make them free.

- 'The year of the Lord's favour': The special time for freedom and joy.

**Luke 4:21.** God has kept his promises! Jesus is God's chosen person, that Isaiah spoke about! Already, Jesus has healed and helped those in physical need. But Jesus has come to bring spiritual freedom from our deepest trouble.

**Luke 4:22, 28, 29.** The people thought that Jesus was a good speaker. But they did not want to believe that their local boy was God's Saviour.

# THE SAVIOUR IS HERE

📖 *Luke 4:16-21*

Describe the meeting. The people have heard about the wonderful things that Jesus has done. Now he has come back to his home town. They really want to hear him speak. He reads from Isaiah and then sits down to speak.

📖 **Luke 4:21**. What a big surprise! Jesus says: 'I am the person in Isaiah!'

⊕ Imagine a man in big trouble. He is blind. He is a prisoner. He has a cruel master who beats him. He cannot escape. He can only hope that someone will come and help him.

For hundreds of years, God's people, Israel, were like that man. God gave them his special land, but they went away from God. God promised to bless them, but their sin took away all the blessing. When Jesus comes, they have their religion, but most are far from God. They need a Saviour to make them free! And God promised this Saviour in Isaiah 61! (In other places in Isaiah, God gives us **many** of these promises.) God will send someone to rescue his people from their sin.

And Jesus looks his listeners in the eyes and says: '**I have come!**'

**This is what Jesus' life was about. He came to save people. He came to make people free from their sin.**

[Talk more about Luke 4:18-19. The notes will help you. When Jesus helped and healed people, he showed his real work. He showed that he is God's Saviour.]

⏩ *The Saviour is here today. Are you in trouble? Are you far from God? Do you need him to open your eyes and make you free? Do you have a cruel master who will not let you go? Jesus looks at you today and says: 'I have come!' He is God's Saviour – he promises to save you if you ask.*

# BELIEVE HIM!

📖 *Luke 4:22, 28-29*

We all like to hear a good speaker! The people all thought Jesus was wonderful! **But they did not want to believe him.** So they tried to kill him!

⏩ *We think that Jesus is a wonderful speaker. We say that his words are good. But Jesus did not come to be a wonderful speaker. He came to **save** us and be our King.*

*Do not only listen to talks about Jesus. Believe him! Ask him to come to make you free. Ask him to rescue you from your sin. That is why he came.*

# 18

# JESUS – CAME TO DIE

## ⦿ Background

Jesus is on his way to Jerusalem. He started this journey in 📖 **Luke 9:51.** He knows that it is a journey to the cross.

This is the only way that Jesus could be the promised Saviour (last TALK). The Saviour has come to die for his people.

### 📖 *Luke 18:31-34*

This is what the prophets said in the Old Testament.

### 📖 *Isaiah 52:13–53:12; Psalm 22*

## ⦿ Main point

Jesus, the promised Saviour, came to die.

## ✶ Things to work on

**1.** This talk (and the next one) is the high point of God's big story. Try to show how exciting this is! Jesus' death is **the answer** to all the problems of sin that we have seen through the Old Testament. It is the only way back into friendship with God. Without Jesus' death, no one has any hope.

**2.** This talk will help people who are not yet true Christians. You could hold a special evangelistic meeting. You could ask one or two believers to tell everyone why the death of Jesus is so important to them. Encourage the Christians to invite their friends to find out why Jesus came.

## ⦿ Notes

**Luke 18:31.** The Old Testament says that the Saviour will **suffer, die** and **rise again.** Jesus knew that this was God's plan for him. At this time, it will all be 'fulfilled' (come true).

**Luke 18:32.** Jesus knew the cruel things that the Roman soldiers would do to him. They would 'mock' (laugh at) him, insult him (say bad things), spit on him and 'flog' (whip) him.

**Luke 18:34.** The disciples could not believe that Jesus was going to die. They did not understand that only his death could save them!

# JESUS CAME TO DIE

📖 *Luke 18:31-33*

⊕ Perhaps you have big plans for your life. What do you **really** want to do?

The disciples had big plans for Jesus' life. He was their great leader. He did so many kind and good things for people. The disciples wanted Jesus to save the nation from all their troubles. They wanted him to be the great King who would lead them in God's ways.

But Jesus did not have big plans for his life. He had big plans for **death**!

Jesus knew just where his journey would end. As he walked closer and closer to Jerusalem, he knew what would happen there. And he went there on purpose. He knew that he must die. That is the reason he came.

**There was no other way to be the promised Saviour. The Saviour must die. This is how he would save his people from their sins.**

⟩⟩ *You cannot be a true Christian unless you trust the Saviour who **died** for you. Jesus is not just an example to follow. He is not just a teacher to listen to. He is the Saviour, who died to take away our sins.*

# AS THE PROPHETS SAID

📖 *Luke 18:31*

God **always** planned for Jesus to die. This was always God's plan to pay the price for sin. The Old Testament talks about this in different ways:

- **The sacrifices**
  📖 *John 1:29.* Israel killed lambs for their sacrifices, but Jesus is the only sacrifice that can truly take away sin. We deserve to die, but Jesus died in our place.

- **The prophecies**
  📖 *Isaiah 53:3-6.* Isaiah tells how Jesus would suffer (like Luke 18:32). See **why** Jesus died. It is because God put **our** sin on Jesus.

This is how God shows his wonderful love for us. He gave his Son to die for us.

📖 **John 3:16. This is God's big answer to the big problem of sin. Jesus' death means that, at last, man can be friends with God again.**

⟩⟩ *Do you realise how bad your sin is? It is so bad that there is only one way to be friends with God again. It is the way that he planned right from the start. **It is the suffering and death of Jesus. Praise God for his wonderful plan!** Think of all the wrong things that you have ever done. You cannot change those things. You cannot make yourself good. But you can bring them all to Jesus. You can trust that his death has paid for every one of them.*

# 19

# JESUS – RISEN

## ⊡ Background

Jesus' resurrection is the final proof. It shows that Jesus certainly **is** the promised Saviour. When Jesus rose from the dead, it showed that:

- Jesus paid the price for sin and God has accepted it.
- Jesus defeated death and Satan.
- Jesus has power to give new life to everyone who believes in him.

📖 *Luke 24:1-49*

## ⊡ Main point

The promised Saviour has risen. Believe it! Praise God!

## ⊠ Something to work on

Decide what your listeners most need to hear. If they already believe the fact that Jesus has risen, talk more about **personal** faith in Jesus. Explain why it is so foolish to believe the facts but not follow the Saviour. Talk about how our lives will change if we really do believe. (We will tell people about Jesus, we will hate sin...)

## ⊡ Notes

**Luke 24:1.** The women wanted to care properly for Jesus' dead body. The 'spices' would help to keep the body fresh.

**Luke 24:4.** These men were angels (Matthew 28:2-6).

**Luke 24:6-7.** See Luke 9:22, 18:31-34. Jesus told the disciples that he would die and rise again. But they did not believe that he would die. And they did not believe that he would rise from the dead. (Luke 24:11)

**Luke 24:13-27.** These men do not believe the women, or the angels. They are sad because Jesus died, and his body has gone! See how Jesus tells them off (rebukes them). They should have listened to the Old Testament! They should have expected the Promised Saviour to die, rise again and go back to heaven. See how Jesus teaches them. He starts at the beginning of the Bible ('Moses'). **All** the Old Testament tells about Jesus, the Promised Saviour.

# JESUS HAS RISEN!

📖 *Luke 24:1-12*

⊕ Your country is going to play against the best team in the world. You know that they cannot win. But you still **hope** that they will!

These women did not even hope like that. They knew for sure that Jesus was dead. They did not even **think** that he might be alive. So they got up early and went to care for Jesus' dead body; 📖 *Luke 24:1.*

The women found no dead body and two live angels! Imagine how scared they were.

📖 *Luke 24:2-5*

Then the angels speak. He has risen! The women must not look for Jesus in a grave. He is alive, not dead!

📖 *Luke 24:5-6*

It does not take long to explain. It is a very simple fact. But it is the most important fact in the world. On that Sunday morning Jesus, the Saviour, rose from the dead. If we had been there, we could have seen the empty grave. We could have met Jesus afterwards, as the disciples did.

⟫ *This is the best thing that ever happened. It means that:*

- *Jesus has paid the price for sin and God has accepted it.*

- *Jesus has defeated death and Satan.*

- *Jesus has power to give new life to everyone who believes in him.*

[Take time to praise God for these wonderful truths.]

# BELIEVE IT!

We should believe in Jesus because of the facts. He rose from the dead. No one could find his dead body. Then Jesus showed himself many times. His risen power changed many lives.

There is another reason why we should believe. **It was always God's plan for Jesus to rise from the dead.** 📖 *Luke 24:6-8* [Tell the story about the two sad disciples (Luke 24:13-27). Why does Jesus rebuke them? Because they should know what the Old Testament Scriptures said! 📖 *Luke 24:25-27.* God told his plan before it happened.]

⟫ *It is hard to believe that someone could rise from the dead. But God told his great plan hundreds of years before it happened. So when it happened, **just as God said**, we should believe!*

*Believe it! But do not only believe the facts. Trust this risen Saviour to take away **your** sin and give you his new life.*

## The Holy Spirit in the Old Testament

God, the Holy Spirit, has always been at work.

In the Old Testament, God's Spirit came to **special people** for **special reasons**.

- For example, God's Spirit came to **David** because he was to be **God's king**; 1 Samuel 16:13.

- God's Spirit came to the **prophets**. He gave them God's words to speak.

The Old Testament promised a time when **all God's people** would have his Spirit; Ezekiel 36:26-27. This is partly how God can now be friends again with man. God's Spirit will come to live in his people.

He came like this **at Pentecost**.

The Holy Spirit is God, as the Father and the Son are God. We talk of him as 'he', not 'it'. The Holy Spirit is not a general force or power. He is not like the sun that affects everyone. He is God, who comes to work in the life of this person or that person.

Only believers have God's Holy Spirit living in them. This is different from our spirit. Our spirit is the part of us that goes on living for ever. It is what God breathed into Adam at the beginning.

## Pentecost

📖 *Acts 2:1-22, 33*

Jesus gives his disciples a great work to do. They must go into the world to take the good news about Jesus to everyone. First Jesus tells them to **wait for the Holy Spirit**. To be God's witnesses, they need power from the Holy Spirit.

📖 *Acts 1:4, 8*

- The day of Pentecost was a **new beginning**. From this day, the Holy Spirit came to believers in a new way.

- **Special things happened** that day. These special things **showed that Jesus had sent his Holy Spirit**. This is what Jesus promised. It is also what the Old Testament promised (Acts 2:16-17).

- The Holy Spirit gave the disciples **power to preach the good news**. Many people believed in Jesus (Acts 2:41).

## The Holy Spirit and Christians

The Holy Spirit works in people who are **not** yet Christians. He shows them their sin and their need of Jesus (John 16:8-11). But he **lives** only in believers.

Jesus said: *'I will ask the Father, and he will give you another Counsellor to be with you for ever – the Spirit of truth … you know him, for he lives with you and will be in you'* (John 14:16-17).

The Holy Spirit is Jesus' gift to **all believers**. He **lives in** all believers. He teaches them **through God's word**. He loves to bring **glory to Jesus**.

## How the Holy Spirit works in Christians' lives

- The Holy Spirit **helps and guides** believers. He **teaches** us truth deep inside. He helps us to **pray** (Romans 8:26).

- The Holy Spirit helps true Christians to be **sure that they are safe**. He tells them that they are God's children (Romans 8:16).

- The Holy Spirit **changes** believers to bring 'fruit' that makes them more like Jesus (Galatians 5:22-23).

- The Holy Spirit does not make it **easy** to live as a Christian. But he does help us in the battle against sin and Satan (Galatians 5:16-17).

- The Holy Spirit gives us **power to tell other people about Jesus**.

## The gifts of the Spirit

- The Spirit gives gifts to every believer.

- There are many different gifts. Every one is God's special gift to us. We must not look down on people who do not have the same gifts (1 Corinthians 12).

- The gifts are for the church. They are not to make us feel good but to serve God's people (Ephesians 4:11-12).

**Important Bible sections:**
John 16:5-16, Romans 8:1-27, Galatians 5:16-26.

*The Holy Spirit is God's very special gift to believers. God tells us to live by the Spirit. He tells us not to make the Spirit sad (Ephesians 4:30). We make God's Spirit sad when we are not careful how we live.*

# JESUS' CHURCH

**20**

## ⊡ Background

Jesus' death and resurrection changed everything. This was the answer to sin. God and man can now be friends. The new family of God's people begins. These are people who believe in Jesus. God changes their hearts so that they want to please God.

Acts tells the exciting story of this new family of Jesus' people, his church; 📖 *Acts 2.*

Peter shows these Jews how Jesus is the promised Saviour. The Holy Spirit comes to change many people. They believe, are baptised and then belong to this new family.

## ⊡ Main point

Christian believers belong to Jesus' family, the church.

## ⊛ Something to work on

Many Christians think that they only need to come to church on Sunday. They think that this is the way to belong to a church. Show that the New Testament picture of a church is a **family**. We might not be able to meet every day as these believers did. But we must follow the way that they **shared their lives**. We help each

other. Jesus wants his new family to follow him **together**.

## ⊡ Notes

**Acts 2:36.** Peter sums up his talk. Jesus is the promised Saviour ('Christ', 'Messiah'). But they killed him on a cross!

**Acts 2:37.** 'cut to the heart'. They had killed their Saviour! They felt their sin so much. It hurt them deep inside.

**Acts 2:38.** God will forgive them when they turn from their sins ('repent'). This does not only mean that we turn from wrong things. It means a **change of heart.** We turn to Jesus. And God gives us new life by his Holy Spirit.

**Acts 2:42-47.** This is a good example of what Jesus' new family is like. Remember that this is a special time. It is a new beginning. Not everything will be the same today.

**Acts 2:41, 47.** When someone believed in Jesus, he did not stay on his own. He joined the new family. Everyone knew that he was a true believer.

# BELIEVE

📖 *Acts 2:36-38*

Believe! This is the only way to belong to Jesus' new family, the church.

- What ways do people **wrongly** think that they can be Christians? (Example: they are born to Christian parents.)

These people **heard the truth** about Jesus. They **felt** their sin. Their **hearts changed** towards Jesus and they turned away from their sin. They knew that Jesus was the promised Saviour, and they asked him to forgive them. And God **gave them his Spirit**. They had God's new life in them.

> 🔊 *You can see their joy in* 📖 *Acts 2:46-47. God has forgiven them! Jesus has made them friends with God! They have his Holy Spirit living in them! You can know this too – believe in Jesus as they did!*

# BAPTISE

📖 *Acts 2:38, 41*

Baptism is the first thing for a new believer to do! This shows that they now belong to Jesus. Another believer baptises them (puts them under water). This is a picture to show that Jesus has washed away their sins. It says to everyone that they are now glad to follow Jesus.

> 🔊 *Do not think that baptism will* **make** *you a Christian. Baptism* **shows** *that you belong to Jesus. It is like a uniform. You wear a uniform to* **show** *that you belong to your school or army. Do you believe? Then be baptised!*

# BELONG

📖 *Acts 2:41-47*

⊕ What is a family like? How should a family care for each other?

New believers belong to Jesus' family. They are now God's children. And they need to join with the family of believers near them (a local church). Jesus does not want his followers to believe in him quietly on their own. We need each other. God wants his family to serve him together.

- What was it like then to belong to Jesus' church family? What did they do?
- Did they like to do things together? What happened if they needed help?
- How can your church family be more like this?

> 🔊 *Are you at the edge of the church? Do you come to meetings, but you do not join in the life of the church family? This is not what Jesus wants! Ask him to help you to change. How can you encourage other members of the church family?*

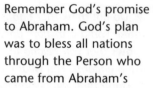

Remember God's promise to Abraham. God's plan was to bless all nations through the Person who came from Abraham's family. It was time for God to keep that promise. God's people must take the good news of Jesus to all nations. The Saviour has come. Everyone who believes in him will be saved.

## The great mission

📖 *Matthew 28:18-20*

Jesus first told his disciples to take the good news round the world. But it is also work for all of Jesus' church family. He gives **us** this special job to do. And it is still not finished!

Acts tells us how God's people began to take the good news to the nations. The plan is in 📖 *Acts 1:8.*

### Acts 1:8 plan
*'You will be my witnesses in* **Jerusalem***, and in all* **Judea and Samaria***, and to the* **ends of the earth***.'*

### 1. Jerusalem

• (Acts calls Jesus' 12 disciples 'apostles'. God made them special leaders over the church.) Peter and the other apostles first preached in Jerusalem (**A** – see MAP). Many Jews believed in Jesus (Acts 6:7).

• Jewish leaders and Herod, the Jewish king, were against the apostles. They put some in prison. Herod killed James. But nothing could stop the apostles. They preached about Jesus and many people believed (Acts 5:41-42).

## 2. Judea and Samaria

• Bad trouble came and the believers had to escape from Jerusalem. They went into **Judea and Samaria** (**B** – see MAP) and told everyone about Jesus! (Acts 8:1, 4-5)

• At first they spoke only to Jews. But God taught Peter (Acts 10) that they must tell the **Gentiles** (people who are not Jews). God's plan is for all nations (Acts 11:18).

## 3. The whole world

• Some Christians travelled further, into Syria (**C**). They began to tell Jews and Gentiles. Many believed (Acts 11:19-21).

• Paul and other missionaries travelled first into Cyprus and Turkey (**D**), then into Europe (**E**). They told Jews and Gentiles the good news. Many churches started to grow. Paul visited the new churches to encourage the believers to carry on (Acts 13-20).

PAUL'S MISSIONARY JOURNEYS

Paul's first journey
Paul's second journey

D Paul's first journey
E Paul's second journey

MACEDONIA

Philippi
Thessalonica
Berea
Athens
Corinth

Troas

ASIA

Ephesus

GALATIA

Tarsus
Derbe
Perga

Cyprus
Paphos

Antioch
SYRIA
C
B Samaria
Caesarea
A Jerusalem

Crete

The Great Sea
(Mediterranean Sea)

# A LETTER TO ENCOURAGE

**21**

The letters help the churches follow Jesus. This is an **example** of a letter.

## ⊡ Background

(See next page for more about the letters.) The new Christians did not have whole Bibles to help them. Paul was only at Thessalonica for a few weeks. Then he had to move to the next place.

### 📖 *Acts 17:1-9*

The new Christians needed help. So, after a while, Paul wrote this letter to encourage them in their faith.

### 📖 *1 Thessalonians 1*

## ⊡ Main point

Be encouraged! Your faith shines out. God has worked in your life.

## ⊞ Something to work on

In this letter, Paul most wants to **encourage** these new believers. But he says other things too. You can mention them. For example, Paul **teaches** them more about how to live (1 Thessalonians 4:1-12). He also **corrects** wrong ideas about when Jesus will come again (1 Thessalonians 4:13 - 5:11).

## ⊡ Notes
**Their new faith clearly shows, in five ways:**

**1 Thessalonians 1:3.** Paul knew that they were true Christians. He had seen their love, faith and hope at work in their lives. Their love and faith made them work for the Lord. Their hope gave them 'endurance' (patience) to carry on when it was hard.

**1 Thessalonians 1:4-5.** Paul also knew that God had chosen them by **the way they received the good news**. The Holy Spirit came with power. He 'convicted' them (convinced them deeply), so that they **knew** that it was true.

**1 Thessalonians 1:6.** They copied ('imitated') Paul's example. Like him and Jesus, they were glad to suffer for their new faith in Jesus.

**1 Thessalonians 1:7.** They then became an example ('model') to Christians in many places.

**1 Thessalonians 1:8-10.** Because they turned from idols, people everywhere talked about the Christians at Thessalonica. The message about Jesus spread because their lives changed so much.

# WHY PAUL WROTE

- When do you find it hard to carry on as a Christian? What things encourage you?

Tell the story of the first time the good news came to Thessalonica (Acts 17:1-9). Show how hard it was to follow Jesus.

Paul tried to visit them again. But things stopped him. Instead, he wrote this letter. Paul knew that the Jews were against the believers. The Jews tried everything to stop them from following Jesus. And Paul really wanted to encourage the Christians!

*» Do you suffer for Jesus? Read the letters! They often encourage Christians to carry on when it is hard. Remember that Christians have always suffered for Jesus. And Jesus has always helped them to carry on (1 Thessalonians 2:14-15).*

# HOW PAUL ENCOURAGED THEM

Talk about the five ways in which the faith of these Christians showed (see notes).

- Their faith, hope and love showed in their lives.
  📖 *1 Thessalonians 1:3*

- The good news came to them with God's power.
  📖 *1 Thessalonians 1:4-5*

- They learned to suffer like Paul and Jesus.
  📖 *1 Thessalonians 1:6*

- They became a good example to other Christians.
  📖 *1 Thessalonians 1:7*

- They spread the good news about Jesus by their life and their words.
  📖 *1 Thessalonians 1:8-10*

*» Think about God's work in your life. Can you see what **God** has done? Thank him! Be encouraged to keep on!*

*How does the example of these Thessalonian Christians help you? Do you want to shine out like them? In what ways will you pray to be more like them? [Pray together at the end about this.]*

*Now think about who **you** can encourage. Perhaps someone who has a hard time. Or someone whose example has helped you.*

It can be hard to keep going as a Christian, but Christians **wait for Jesus to come**.
📖 *1 Thessalonians 1:10.* Then all the pain will seem like nothing.

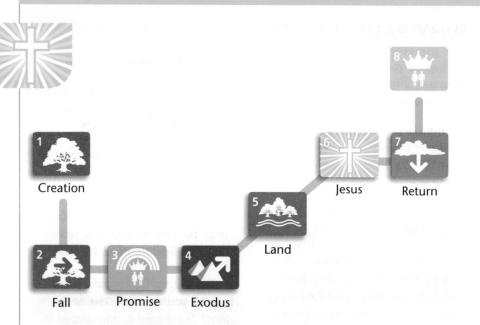

**Think about the story of God's family.**

Promise

Sin separates man from God, but this is not the end. God **promises** Abraham more people than the stars in the sky. These people will come from all nations.

Land

God brings his people out of Egypt into the Promised **Land**. God blesses them. But they worship false gods. Sin continues to separate God's family from God. They need a Saviour to save them from their sin.

Jesus

The Saviour comes and dies to take away sin. This is the only way for man to be friends with God. People from all nations hear about **Jesus** and believe. They are God's new family. God gives them new hearts so that they are willing friends with God.

But the story is not finished. God's people are not yet **home** with God. They wait for Jesus to return to take them home. Until then, they live in a world that is against them. It is hard to live as God's friends. How do they keep going?

They have God's **Spirit**, God's **people** and God's **word**...

## The letters

God speaks to Christians through the letters. They teach us how to live **now** as we wait for Jesus to return.

When Paul and the other apostles wrote their letters, the believers did not have a New Testament to teach them. They had many difficulties to face. They needed the letters to help them to live as Christians.

## How the letters help Christians

- **The letters encourage Christians to keep going.** People often attack Christians for their faith. There are many difficulties to go through. The letters say: 'It is usual to suffer. We follow a Saviour who suffered'.

- **The letters put right Christians' mistakes.** Sometimes Christians start to believe false teaching. The letters put these things right, so that God's family follows the truth.

- **The letters teach Christians how to live.** People round us live in wrong ways. It is hard not to follow their example. The letters teach us that we are new people. We have a new way to live. We please God, not ourselves.

## Who wrote the letters?

**Paul** wrote nine letters in the Bible to **churches** (Romans to 2 Thessalonians). He also wrote letters to encourage **workers** (Timothy and Titus), and a personal letter to **Philemon**.

Other apostles (**James, Peter, Jude** and **John**) wrote to encourage Christians in hard times.

We do not know who wrote **Hebrews**.

## How to understand the letters

- Read the letter through a few times. Why does the writer say what he says? This will help you to understand what the problems were in the church. What are the main things that the writer wants them to hear? Write down words that he repeats a few times.

- How are we like that church? How are our difficulties like theirs? How does the letter speak to us today?

### Example: Colossians

Paul repeats 'fill' 'fullness' 'complete'. False teachers talked about new, better experiences. Paul shows that we have **everything** that we need in Jesus.

# 22 JESUS' RETURN

## ◉ Background

Christians wait for Jesus to come back (1 Thessalonians 1:10). Jesus will take them home. At last, all God's promises will come true. Jesus will be King in a perfect world that nothing can spoil.

**All** of the New Testament teaches a lot about Jesus' return. We will look at Jesus' own words.

### 📖 Matthew 24

Before our section (Matthew 24:29-44), Jesus teaches that:

- Trouble will always come. Perhaps a big flood or earthquake. That does not mean that the end of the world is near (Matthew 24:6-8).

- The good news will go to all the world before Jesus returns (Matthew 24:14).

- Jesus will come after a time of very great trouble (Matthew 24:21).

## ◉ Main point

Jesus **will** return to bring his people home. Be ready for him!

## ✴ Something to work on

Do not miss the point! People have many questions about Jesus' return.

The important thing is to believe it and to be ready! Preach this clearly.

## ◉ Notes

**Matthew 24:29.** This is from the prophet Isaiah. Our world will begin to break, as things go wrong in the sky. The world will end in fire when Jesus comes (2 Peter 3:10).

**Matthew 24:30.** 'mourn' ('weep') = cry. 📖 **Revelation 6:12-17.** Everyone who does not know Jesus will cry in fear. They are not ready to meet him.

**Matthew 24:31.** His 'elect' are his chosen people. They trust in Jesus.

**Matthew 24:34.** This 'generation'. This could mean 'race'; the Jewish people. Or, Jesus may mean the 'generation' of people who are alive **when the last signs come**. He will return before those people die.

**Matthew 24:36.** Even Jesus did not know when he would return. (This is because Jesus set limits to what he knew. He was a real man.) 'No one knows.' People who say that they know when Jesus will come are **wrong**! Do not believe them.

# JESUS WILL RETURN

📖 *Matthew 24:29-31*

⊞ When something big happens in the world, many people see it on their televisions. But some people miss it.

**No one** will miss Jesus' return. People who are asleep will wake up. Jesus will shine so brightly in the sky. The trumpets (instruments) will sound so loud. Everyone will see Jesus. He will come with power. 📖 *Matthew 24:27, 30*

And **everyone** will know who Jesus is. People everywhere will cry in fear. They will want to hide, but they will not be able to. No one will be able to escape from his glory.

Believers in Jesus will not be afraid. He has come for them! He has come to collect his chosen people and take them home with him. 📖 *Matthew 24:31*

⟫ *There will be terrible times for Christians before Jesus comes back. But if you trust in Jesus, **do not be afraid** of the end of the world. Soon you will be with Jesus in a new wonderful world.*

# BE READY!

📖 *Matthew 24:36-44*

Not many things are certain, but this one is sure. Jesus **will** return, as he says. Believe his words. 📖 *Matthew 24:35*

So the important thing is to **be ready**. 📖 *Matthew 24:44*

People thought Noah was silly to build his boat. They laughed at him. They carried on with their lives. They enjoyed themselves and did not listen to God. They said that everything would go on, as it always had done. **Then God judged them with the flood.**

- Are people like that today? Do they take no notice of God's warnings?

- Are you like that? Will you be ready for Jesus?

⟫ *Two people will be in church when Jesus comes back. Two people will be at work in the fields. Jesus will take one of them home. The other one will be left behind. Jesus will judge him. Which one will you be?*

**How can we be ready?**

We need to **belong** to Jesus' family. We must **trust** him to be our Saviour. Then we can **pray** for Jesus to come back. And we must not be lazy and live for ourselves. When Jesus returns, he wants to find us at **work** for him.

📖 *2 Peter 3:10-13*

89

# 23 JUDGEMENT DAY

## ⊡ Background

When Jesus returns, **everyone** who has died will rise from the dead. They will have new bodies. Then everyone who has ever lived will meet Jesus, their Judge.

### 📖 John 5:25-29

Jesus used a picture to help us to understand Judgement Day. A farmer let the sheep and goats feed in the same field in the daytime. At night, he separated the sheep from the goats. On Judgement Day, Jesus will separate his people ('sheep') from everyone else (the 'goats').

### 📖 Matthew 25:31-46

## ⊡ Main point

Jesus will judge everyone when he returns. He will bring his people home with him. He will send everyone else away to hell.

## ✴ Something to work on

Jesus will judge us by **what we have done**. The Bible teaches this in many places (Psalm 62:12, 2 Corinthians 5:10, Revelation 20:12). The Bible also teaches that only **faith in Jesus** will save us (John 3:36, Ephesians 2:8-9).

These two things fit together because **what we do** shows if we **believe in Jesus**. If Jesus has saved us, he changes our hearts so that we love to serve him. Remember that when Jesus judges us, he looks at our hearts, not only the good things themselves (Matthew 7:21-23).

## ⊡ Notes

**Matthew 25:34.** Notice that this was God's plan right from the beginning. At creation, God planned this new kingdom for his people. ('Inheritance' is God's gift of heaven.)

**Matthew 25:40.** This does not mean that anyone who helps poor people will go to heaven. Notice that these people help Jesus' **'brothers'**, which means Christians. The most important thing is that they help other people **for Jesus**. Jesus sees their **love for him**.

# JESUS WILL JUDGE

📖 *Matthew 25:31-33*

⊕ What is the biggest crowd of people that you have ever seen? Now think of everyone in the whole world. Think too of all the people who have died, and on Judgement Day will rise from the dead. Everyone will be there. You will be there.

📖 *Matthew 25:31-33*

On that day, everyone looks at Jesus, their Judge. He shines with glory. Angels are round him. Jesus sits on his throne (king's seat), as King and Judge. Then he separates that big crowd into two groups. He knows everyone. He knows who the 'sheep' are – and who the 'goats' are. He knows who belongs to him. He knows who has never known him.

# TWO KINDS OF LIVES 📖 *Matthew 25:35-45*

Jesus knows us better than we know ourselves. He sees everything that we ever **do**, and **say**, and **think**. He knows **why** we do the things we do. He knows what we **want**.

➤ *What does Jesus see in your life? Does he see things like*
📖 *Matthew 25:35-36?*

*Does he see that you serve **him** and love **him**? You do many things for many people, but you do them because you love Jesus!*

➤ *Or does he see*
📖 *Matthew 25:42-43?*

*Perhaps you only live to please yourself, not Jesus. Perhaps you do many good things for people, but never for Jesus!*

# TWO PLACES

📖 *Matthew 25:34, 41, 46*

'**Come to me!**' 📖 *Matthew 25:34.* What wonderful words! God has prepared a kingdom for us to enjoy with him for ever! God has blessed us so much if we know Jesus.

'**Go away from me!**' 📖 *Matthew 25:41.* Those are the worst words that we could ever hear. We are under God's **curse** if we have never lived for Jesus. He will **punish** us because we did not want him. There will be **pain for ever**. We will go away from God, but we will be **with the devil** and evil spirits.

➤ 📖 *1 John 4:17-18. You can be confident if you know Jesus' love! You do not need to be afraid of Judgement Day.*

*But if you are not ready to meet Jesus, you need to get ready **now**. Ask Jesus to forgive you. Ask him to change you. Ask him to help you to serve **him** now.*

**91**

We have seen how God uses **different kinds** of Bible writing to tell us his big story. (See pages 10-11.)

- **History** tells us what happened.

- **Songs and wise words** give wisdom to think about. Their poetry expresses feelings well.

- **Prophecy** bring God's direct words. God warns and gives hope.

- **Letters** speak to Christians who, like us, need help to live for God.

**Revelation** is another kind of writing. It is very different to all the other types of writing. We do not read this kind of writing in books today. This makes it hard to understand.

Revelation is a 'vision'. John sees things in his dreams which he then writes down. So he speaks in **vision language**. His dreams are like pictures which have a meaning.

Parts of Daniel, Ezekiel and Zechariah are also like this.

### Example: In Revelation 12:3, John sees a red dragon.

The **dragon** (a fierce animal in stories) is a good picture of the **devil**. It tells us more than the word 'devil'. 'Dragon' shows how dangerous and angry the devil is.

The dragon has 10 **horns**.

Horns are a picture of power or kings. The devil has a lot of power.

## How do we know what the pictures mean?

This is not easy, but do not guess!

- Often the pictures come from the **Old Testament**. A study Bible will help you to find them.

### Example: We know that the dragon means the devil because Revelation 12:9 says so.

We know that horns mean power or kings because the **Old Testament** uses this picture. My study Bible refers to Daniel 7. There is a dragon with 10 horns. The 10 horns are 10 kings (Daniel 7:24).

- John often uses a picture more than once in **Revelation**. Find the other places to help you understand the picture.

The dreams often use **numbers**. These numbers are also pictures. Each number **means** something.

### Example: There are 144,000 people with the 'Lamb' in heaven (Revelation 7:4-8, 14:1).

This comes from 12,000 from each of the 12 tribes of Israel. 12 is a number that means 'complete' – there is no one missing. 12,000 is a large, complete number.

So 144,000 is not the actual number of people in heaven (Revelation 7:9). 144,000 means the big, complete number of God's people from all his 'tribes'.

## What is the message?

It is very important to think about the people who John **first wrote to**. Always ask, 'How did **they** understand this?' This will help **us** to know how we should understand it. (For example, we will not try to fit events today with verses in Revelation. The people then would never have understood it like that!)

The Christians then **suffered a lot for their faith**. They would not worship the Roman king (Caesar), so he killed many Christians. Caesar had power over the world. It seemed that he could do whatever he liked.

The message of Revelation is that **God is the real King**. God is in charge of the world. Caesar, or any human power today, is **not** in charge. Everything happens to fit in with God's great plan. The devil is strong and angry. Many Christians lose their lives. **But God wins.** God's people are safe for ever.

Revelation uses vision language to show:

- **the battle on earth**. God's people have great trouble but **God is in control**.
- **the battle in heaven**. Satan fights against God, but this is also in **God's plan**.

## What happens in the end?

God wins. Jesus returns to defeat Satan for one last time. Jesus judges the world, which has been against his people. He throws all his enemies into hell.

**And everyone who trusts in Jesus goes home to be with him for ever.**

So the Bible ends. God's big story ends with a wonderful new beginning.

# 24 NEW CREATION!

## ◉ Background

At last! God will keep all his promises to Abraham. God's people, from all nations, will be with him for ever. They will have perfect new bodies. They will have no sin. They will live in a new place like the Garden of Eden, but even better. (When we say 'heaven' we should think of 'a new heaven and a new **earth**'.) Satan and all God's enemies will be in hell. Sin will never again come in and separate man from God.

God's story has a very happy ending for everyone who trusts in Jesus. In fact it is a new **beginning** that never ends!

## 📖 Revelation 20:11 – 21:27

## ◉ Main point

God has a perfect new home land for his people. There they will live with him for ever as his friends.

## ◉ Something to work on

It is hard to think what this new home land will be like. It will be much **better** than anything that we can imagine. Remind your listeners that we will have real bodies and real lives. Think of the best things about this world. Think of the best times that you enjoy with people.

Our new world will be much better! Friendships in our new home will be perfect. Best of all, we will be perfect friends with Jesus.

## ◉ Notes

**Revelation 21:1.** 'no sea' ('vanished' means gone). This does not mean there are no lakes in heaven. This is picture language! The Bible often connects sea with evil (Revelation 13:1). Seas also separate people.

**Revelation 21:2.** More picture language. The city, 'Jerusalem' is also a 'bride' at the same time! Both are pictures, not of heaven itself, but of God's people, the church. They show how beautiful and perfect God's people will be (Revelation 21:9-27).

**Revelation 21:6.** 'Alpha and Omega' are the first and last Greek letters (like A and Z in English). Jesus began God's big story and he will end it.

**Revelation 21:6-7.** 'thirsty'. See Revelation 22:17. See how the water of eternal life is free for anyone who wants it! We can come to Jesus and ask him to save us ('drink' from him). Then we keep trusting Jesus to 'overcome' (win against sin and Satan). And God will be our Father for ever.

## NEW HOME

 *Revelation 21:1*

This world is spoilt and broken. It is under the curse of sin. God will end it with fire. But God has a new home for his people, as he promised. It will be so much better than the Promised Land! It will even be better than the Garden of Eden!

• Think of all the good things on this earth. Everything will be much better in this new heaven and new earth!

## NEW PEOPLE

 *Revelation 21:2*

No one will spoil the new home! God will make his people new too, with new bodies and no sin.

• Think about the two pictures of the 'new Jerusalem' and the lovely bride dressed for Jesus. What do they teach us about how God's people will be?

## NEW FRIENDSHIP

 *Revelation 21:3*

If we know Jesus, we are friends with God now. But God is still in heaven and we are on earth. Sin comes between us and God, and spoils our friendship.

• What will be different in our new home?

• Think about being so close to God!

What will that be like? What friends we will be!

## NEW EVERYTHING

 *Revelation 21:4-7*

• Think of all the things that spoil our world. They will not be there in our new home!

Our new home will work in a completely new way to this world. Nothing will go wrong. Everything will be new and good. This is because God is King. His rule will be happy and perfect. Imagine it!

> ⟫ *Does this excite you? Do you want to be there? You can be, if you...*
>
> • *drink the free water of life! If you are thirsty to know Jesus, he will forgive you. He will welcome you into his kingdom of heaven.*  *Revelation 22:17*
>
> • *keep on to the end.*  *Revelation 21:7. Heaven is not for people who say that they believe in Jesus and then forget him. True believers fight on to the end.*

God's big story has a very happy ending for everyone who trusts in Jesus! And our new home is only the **beginning** of a life that is too good to imagine. [Pray and sing songs to God. Praise him for all the wonderful things about our new home.]

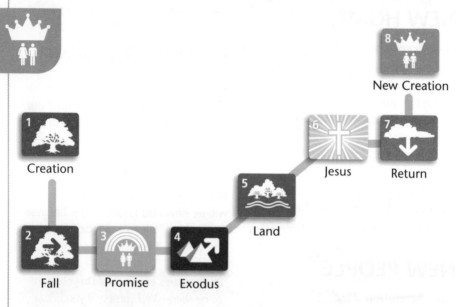

Creation

New Creation

Jesus       Return

Land

Fall       Promise       Exodus

A good way to remember Gods big story is **people, presence, place**. (Presence means that God is **with us**.)

Creation

**God makes everything good.**
God's **people** (Adam and Eve) enjoy his **presence** in his **place** (Eden). Then sin and Satan spoil everything.

Promise

**God promises Abraham that he will bless people from all nations.** One day, God's **people** will again enjoy God's **presence** in his **place**. God gives Israel the Promised Land, but sin spoils this too.

Jesus

**Jesus dies and rises again to defeat sin and Satan.**
Now **people** from all over the world can be friends with God. They enjoy Jesus' rule over them. But they have to wait for the rest of God's promise.

New Creation

**King Jesus will return to bring his people home.** There will be no more sin. Satan will be sent to hell. God's **people** will enjoy God's **presence** for ever in the perfect **place**. Praise God!